30119 025 697 09 7

D0715536

WAL

NAVIGATING WITH A GPS

EFFECTIVE SKILLS FOR THE OUTDOORS

ABOUT THE AUTHOR

Pete Hawkins has been teaching walkers to navigate for over 23 years. His first GPS still works despite its location freezing on the car park of a pub during a recording for BBC Radio 4! With two successful books on using maps and compasses under his belt this is his first foray into writing about GPS navigation.

Pete lives and works in the Peak District National Park where he runs Peakland Walking Holidays and Silva-sponsored Map and Compass Courses.

Other Cicerone books by the author
Map and Compass: The art of navigation
Navigation: Techniques and skills for walkers

NAVIGATING WITH A GPS

EFFECTIVE SKILLS FOR THE OUTDOORS

by

Pete Hawkins

2 POLICE SQUARE, MILNTHORPE, CUMBRIA LA7 7PY
www.cicerone.co.uk

First edition 2008
ISBN-13: 978 1 85284 491 2

© Pete Hawkins 2008

All photos and illustrations by the author unless credited otherwise.

The author asserts his moral right to be identified as the author of this work. All rights reserved.

A catalogue record for this book is available from the British Library.

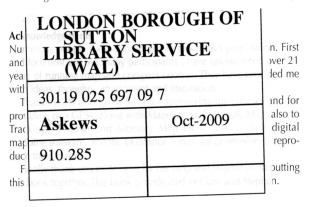

**LONDON BOROUGH OF SUTTON
LIBRARY SERVICE
(WAL)**

30119 025 697 09 7	
Askews	Oct-2009
910.285	

ols Ordnance Survey® This product includes mapping data licensed from Ordnance Survey® with the permission of the Controller of Her Majesty's Stationery Office.
© Crown copyright 2008. All rights reserved.
Licence number PU100012932

CONTENTS

PREFACE

The skill that separates us from the rest of the animal kingdom – apart, perhaps, from stick-wielding chimpanzees – is our ability to shape and control our environment with technology. Whether that technology always works to our benefit, and whether we are capable of using it sensibly, is open to debate, but there is no doubt that the rate of technological change in recent years has been immense.

I remember talking to my grandfather the day after the first moon landing on 20 July 1969. Born at the start of the 20th century, he told me that if he died then and there he'd go happily, having seen it all. The advances during his lifetime radically shaped the human landscape – cars, radio, television, finally being able to land on another planet – but the rate of change since then has been staggering. Although some may feel that our lives are now controlled by technology to the extent that when it doesn't work we can neither work nor play, it's important to recognise that it has brought about major advances in many fields.

In the outdoor world too we have benefitted from the march of progress. Our gear has become more technical, from the development of breathable and wickable fabrics to clothing that absorbs our excess heat and stores it until we need it.

But it is in the field of navigation where, literally, space-age technology has brought us tremendous possibilities. The price of Global Positioning Satellite (GPS) receivers has dropped rapidly over recent years (as their accuracy has increased) and it seems as if everyone is now talking about them. What used to be a toy for those with money to burn has now become a commonplace gadget on the hills and mountains of the world.

On the face of it that's fine. Here we have a technology that is now accurate to a few metres and can pinpoint your location anywhere on earth within seconds. It can supply the user with a mass of helpful information whether he is walking to the South Pole or through the leafy lanes of Surrey.

And therein lies the problem. Sophisticated as they are, GPS receivers are rarely used to their full capacity, whilst still be relied upon to the detriment of other essential navigational skills. They are either expensive ways of calculating grid references or are treated as an infallible oracle, with the user forever staring into the screen-of-wisdom looking for insight.

The aim of this guidebook is simple: to show the user how he or she can get the most from a GPS without becoming totally reliant on it for navigation. The book will also look at the way GPS integrates with other technologies, in particular digital mapping software, which enables the user to plan a route on screen before downloading it to the GPS.

Pete Hawkins, 2008

Note So far I've used the phrase Global Positioning Satellite (GPS) with or without the word 'receiver', a clumsy description for the box of tricks available from your local outdoor shop. Through the power of Western marketing (see Chapter 1) the term GPS has become a generic acronym to describe all receiving units that translate the weak radio signals emitted from scores of satellites into a location. The Russian system, and the much newer European system, will probably be saddled with the American acronym forever, as will this book (for ease of understanding). If that upsets the purist, I apologise.

CHAPTER 1
Introduction

Satellites and GPS technology

When my grandfather sat watching Neil Armstrong make his historic
'small step', the idea that in just a few years' time we would be using
satellites to navigate our way round the world was probably no more
than a pipe dream in some scientist's brain. Those pioneering astro-
nauts got to the moon without satellite navigation – almost
unimaginable for those of us who switch on our in-car sat-navs just
to get to the shops!

The origin of the current system dates back to the late 1970s when
the Americans launched 24 satellites that circle the earth twice a day.
These emit a weak radio signal that GPS receivers employ to calculate the user's exact location. The idea is very simple. By calculating
the difference between when the signal was sent and when it was
received, the GPS receiver can calculate the satellite's location.

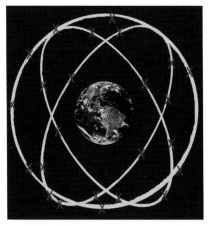

Figure 1.1
*The American GPS
system uses 24 satellites
that circle the earth on
regular orbits*

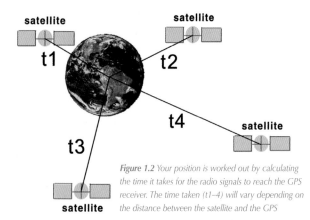

Figure 1.2 Your position is worked out by calculating the time it takes for the radio signals to reach the GPS receiver. The time taken (t1–4) will vary depending on the distance between the satellite and the GPS

Once the receiver has signals from three satellites, it can calculate its own location in 2D (latitude and longitude). With four or more satellites it can work out altitude as well. The early receivers could only accept signals from a maximum of six satellites, but modern units can lock onto up to 16 satellites at any one time.

GPS – Global Positioning System – was developed for American military uses. The satellites were programmed to send out a random error to civilian users, which limited the accuracy of the location to around 150m. When America was involved in military conflict, this 'selective availability' (SA) was switched off, so their bombers could, presumably, bomb more accurately.

In the year 2000 – following the development of technology with which the Americans could confuse enemy GPSs – SA was permanently switched off; suddenly our GPS receivers were accurate to within 15m. This coincided with a sharp reduction in the price of receivers and they became a far more common sight on the hills and mountains of the world.

GPS accuracy is good, but there are situations where it isn't good enough. Airline pilots, for example, currently are not allowed to land using GPS in poor visibility, because the system is not precise enough.

A secondary system which checks the accuracy of the circling satellites is necessary, and comes in the form of a number of geostationary satellites and a series of ground stations. The American system is called WAAS (Wide Area Augmentation System) and the European EGNOS (European Geostationary Navigation Overlay Service). GPSs within an area covered by these ground stations are accurate to 2 or 3m. Newer GPSs can pick up these signals; the display will indicate in some way that this is happening (Figure 1.3). Even if you're picking up EGNOS signals, most units will tell you that you're registering WAAS ones.

Figure 1.3 GPS showing that WAAS signal is being picked up

Over the next few years – funding permitting – the European 'GPS' system, Galileo, will be coming on stream. This will be a series of 30 satellites covering the whole globe. Galileo will work in tandem with the American system and the lesser-known Russian one (GLONASS) and will mean our GPSs will soon be accurate to around 1m.

The technological implications of this are many (and beyond the scope of this book) and will be far more exciting than the navigational kit we currently play with on the hills and in our cars. Expect some stunning developments over the next few years.

Using GPS receivers

There is a huge range of GPS receivers aimed at walkers and other outdoor enthusiasts currently on the market, as well as units aimed at motorists, either built in to the vehicle or removable, and crossover GPSs that have 'sat-nav' programmes for motorists but can also run software more suited for outdoor navigation – on which this book will focus.

GPSs for the outdoor enthusiast (with or without on-screen Ordnance Survey mapping) are designed to help get you from A to B (and perhaps help you identify exactly where A and B are!). In doing so a GPS will bombard you with masses of extra information which you may or may not want. Speed, average speed, altitude, bearing you should be taking, track (the actual bearing you're walking on), the distance you are from the correct route, and so on. We'll look at these in greater detail in later chapters.

The added benefit of GPSs is the fact that they can link with digital mapping software on your computer. Used together these become an invaluable planning and analysis tool. You can plan a route in advance, follow the route on the GPS and analyse the actual route you walked later on your computer.

Chapter 2 discusses what the information on a GPS display means, and encourages you to read the instruction manual so you know how your particular machine works. Chapters 4 and 5 go through the essentials of navigating with a GPS, starting with the most elementary skills and building to more complicated routines as you become more confident. There are practical exercises throughout the book, giving you an opportunity to reflect on what you've read and put those skills into practice.

GPSs are little computers, and there are occasions when they can fail. Chapter 6 looks at the steps you need to consider should this happen, whether you have to reboot the unit, replace the batteries or resort to traditional navigation skills (the latter are covered in Chapter 3, which also looks at how your GPS can be used to replicate these methods).

The final two chapters introduce digital mapping and look at how these can be used to enhance your developing GPS skills, and how to keep these new-found skills honed.

This is not a 'quick-read-and-become-an-expert' book. Take your time to try the exercises practically and develop your skills and you'll emerge a confident and effective GPS navigator.

First things first: let's get to grips with what your GPS is telling you.

CHAPTER 2
What GPSs Show You

Wander into any outdoor shop and take a look at the GPS receivers on show: you'll find a bewildering range of units for sale. The common makes for walkers are Garmin and Magellan, with Lowrance, Satmap and Memory Map's Road Angel coming up fast behind. Each manufacturer and unit has different displays and layouts, and reproducing them here would turn this pocket book into a mammoth tome. It would also be unnecessary because I'm not going to tell you how to use your individual unit – your user manual will do that. Instead I want to tell you how to *navigate* with your GPS and – whilst some receivers are more complicated than others – the basic navigational skills are the same for all GPSs.

At this point it's worth taking a look at some of the common terms used by GPS receivers. Different manufacturers may use slightly varying terms, but the following list details the most common.

Term	Explanation
Altitude	Your height above sea level – needs four or more satellites.
Average Speed	A constantly changing average reading of your speed – quickly drops to zero when you stop.
Bearing	As with a compass, this is the angle from north that takes you from where you are to where you want to go.
Cross Track or Xtrack	Distance to the left or right that you are off route.
EPE	Estimated Position Error is an estimation by the GPS of the accuracy of the readings you are receiving.
ETA	Estimated Time of Arrival is based on your current speed and distance from your destination.

Term	Explanation
Heading	Compass direction in which you are currently travelling. Unlike the bearing, the heading is temporary.
POI	Points of Interest. Many GPSs come ready loaded with masses of 'useful' POIs. Great if you're looking for your nearest petrol station or fast food restaurant; less so if you're using your unit to navigate the hills and mountains. It is usually possible to add your own POIs to the list.
Position	Your current location (in latitude or longitude or in the local grid system: for example, OSGB36 indicates the British Grid).
Route	A file of linked waypoints saved in your GPS unit or computer.
Speed or Ground Speed	The speed you are travelling at any given time.
Track	The route you have followed to get to your current location, recorded by a series of waypoints automatically logged by the GPS. It can be transferred to mapping programs on your computer for an exact plot of your route.
UTM	Universal Transverse Mercator is a global grid system that divides topographic maps into 1km squares for easy and accurate plotting. It is starting to replace latitude and longitude as the standard for modern land navigation.
WAAS	Wide Area Augmentation System is a network of ground stations that work with GPS satellites to enhance signal accuracy.
Waypoint	Electronic pinpoint of a place.

Note Of all the data a GPS produces the altitude figure is going to be the least accurate, for two reasons. Firstly the geodetic datum (OSGB36 for the British Isles) assumes that the earth is a perfect sphere, which it isn't. The second explanation which compounds the error is that because the satellites used by the GPS are all above the horizon (line of sight) the resultant geometric calculation is prone to error. The GPS would need to use data from satellites below the horizon for greater accuracy (which it cannot do because it cannot 'see' them).

Every GPS unit will give you a range of information on a variety of screens which you can scroll through.

1 Most will give an indication of how many satellites your unit can 'see', and the strength of the signal (Figure 2.1).

2 Your unit's battery life, whether the unit is giving you 2D or 3D readings, and whether the WAAS signals are being picked up.

Figure 2.1 *GPS showing the number of satellites picked up, and signal strength, as well as the remaining battery life*

Figure 2.2 OS map on a GPS screen

Figure 2.3 Simplified mapping screen typical of many GPS units

3 You'll get some form of graphical representation of your position, either in the form of a Ordnance Survey map on screen (Figure 2.2) or a simplified map, maybe showing the road network (Figure 2.3), or a simpler screen representing your location which will then indicate your route once you start moving (Figure 2.4).

4 You should get a screen that indicates the direction you need to go in when heading for a waypoint (Figure 2.5).

Figure 2.4 Very simple location and route screen

5 There will also be a screen that summarises your location with a grid reference (or latitude and longitude, depending on how you've set up your GPS – check in the user manual), and shows the time and date (Figure 2.6).

Some GPSs give additional information. My Lowrance Expedition GPS gives me a barometric pressure reading, an indication of the weather based on the change in barometric pressure over time, and even the ability to play music files! Bear in mind that the more you flip through the pages, play MP3s or have the various features activated, the quicker the batteries will run down. I always have my electronic compass switched off when battery life is critical.

If you haven't already given your instruction manual a good read through do so now and make yourself familiar with the workings of your particular GPS. If you are planning to use it on the hill you will need to navigate your way round your GPS efficiently and understand what the information screens are telling you.

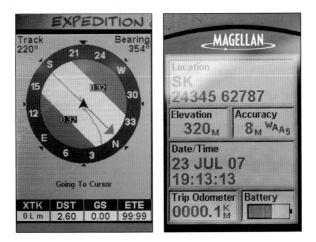

Figure 2.5 Direction screen   **Figure 2.6** Location summary

Why use a GPS on the hill?

The arrival of the GPS in the outdoor world has sparked a debate between the traditionalists and the 'techies': do GPSs add anything to the art of navigation? The following positive and negative points may help you decide where you stand.

Plus points
- GPSs provide a quick and accurate position fix.
- GPSs provide additional useful information such as your walking speed, the track you're heading on, altitude and so on.
- GPSs enable you to walk off your bearing (for example round obstacles), but will guide you to your intended destination.
- GPSs are best used in conjunction with a map.
- GPSs are fun to play with.

But beware...
- GPSs should never be used as your sole means of navigation.
- GPSs are mini computers and can stop working for a variety of reasons.
- GPSs have problems picking up signals in thick woodland, around high cliffs or in deep valleys.

Having a thorough grasp of your GPS's functions is important, but so is the ability to navigate properly with a map and a compass. Whatever information your GPS provides should always be crossed-checked on the map; should the unit fail you will have to resort to using map and compass. The next chapter leads you though the essential map and compass skills and looks at how a GPS can be used to replicate or enhance the conventional information.

> *Practical exercise*
> Learn all about your GPS. Read the manual carefully. Take your GPS for short walks to see how things work and what the different screens are telling you. Learn how to enter waypoints, check grid references, how to tell your unit to navigate to a point and so on.

CHAPTER 3

Building Navigation Skills: Using a Map and Compass

In the early days of GPS I often heard the cry that map and compass skills were dead. Much of the manufacturers' advertising backed this up, and at one time it seemed that the only objectors were old traditionalists. Happily things have changed and the message you'll get when buying a GPS today is that you should never totally rely on it. GPSs are a useful adjunct to traditional navigation skills, and are handy tools in many situations on the hill, but it is important to understand that they are neither failsafe nor a complete replacement for map and compass.

So before we look further at the practicalities of navigating with GPS let's take a lightning tour of the essential map and compass skills. I would suggest, however, that if you are not 100 percent happy with using your map and compass on the hill in poor weather it is unwise to rely solely on a GPS. The sister title to this book – *Navigation: Techniques and skills for walkers* – will help you to brush up your skills, as will the many practical courses held in the UK every year (see Appendix I).

Understanding maps

Maps come in a range of scales, the commonest for walkers being 1:25,000 and 1:50,000. Most walkers prefer the 1:25,000 scale as it contains much more detail and as a result navigation can be more accurate (see Figures 3.1a & b). A scale is a ratio of the distance on the map to the distance on the ground: 1cm on a 1:25,000 map represents 25,000cm or 250m on the ground.

> **Note** GPSs that display OS mapping will show it at whatever scale you choose to upload, but it is possible to zoom in or out of those maps. This won't give you more or less detail but will, if you zoom in for example, enable you to check on the fine details that might not be very clear at the printed scale (see Figures 3.2a–c).

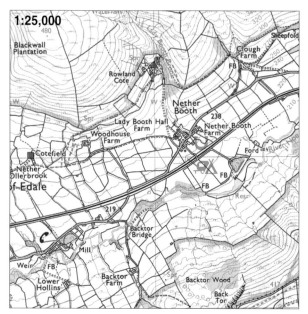

Figure 3.1a

Figures 3.1a & b
The same area of the map shown
at two different scales:
(a) 1:25,000 (above) and
(b) 1:50,000 (right)

Figure 3.1b

Figures 3.2a–c
*Zooming in gives you a
bigger map but no more
detail*

Figure 3.2a

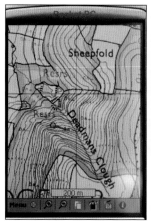

Figure 3.2b

Figure 3.2c

Grid lines and references

The standard format for a UK grid reference is given as SK 123 456. To understand what this means we need to break it down into its various elements.

Adorning every map is a grid of vertical and horizontal lines. These enable any location in the UK to be given a unique reference known as a grid reference. The UK grid lines originate from an artificial grid of 25 x 500km squares drawn over the country. These squares are labelled A–Z, omitting the letter I. Each of these large squares is further subdivided into another 25 x 100km squares lettered A–Z, again omitting I. These two sets of squares give the lettered part of a grid reference, for example SK.

The number section of the grid reference is obtained from the grid lines on your map, which are subdivisions of the smaller lettered squares broken down into kilometre squares numbered 1–99 from west to east. To construct the number section of a grid reference use the numbers along the bottom or top of the map first, followed by the numbers up the side. Because the numbered squares are repeated every 100km the grid letters are used to make a grid reference a unique location.

The map extract in Figure 3.3 shows a small area of the Peak District. How do you work out the grid reference of the footpath junction labelled A?

Figure 3.3 (right)
Map extract showing
footpath junction A

Figure 3.4a (opposite
above) Extract from map
key showing which grid
squares the map covers
Figure 3.4b (opposite
below) Extract showing
how the grid letters are
also included on the map

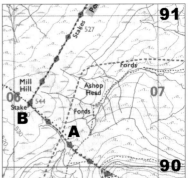

THE NATIONAL GRID REFERENCE SYSTEM

Base map constructed on Transverse Mercator Projection, Airy Spheroid, OSGB (1936) Datum.
Vertical datum mean sea level (Newlyn)

The grid lines form part of the National Grid and are at 1 km intervals.
To give a unique reference position of a point to within 100 metres proceed as follows:

SAMPLE POINT: Moorside Farm

1. Read letters identifying 100 000 metre square in which the point lies..... SJ

2. FIRST QUOTE EASTINGS
   Locate first VERTICAL grid line to LEFT of point and read LARGE figures
   labelling the line either in the top or bottom margin or on the line itself....... 99
   Estimate tenths from grid line to point..5

3. AND THEN QUOTE NORTHINGS
   Locate first HORIZONTAL grid line BELOW point and read LARGE figures
   labelling the line either in the left or right margin or on the line itself.................97
   Estimate tenths from grid line to point.................5

SAMPLE REFERENCE   SJ 995975
For local referencing grid letters may be omitted

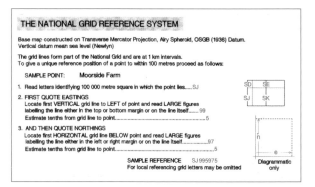

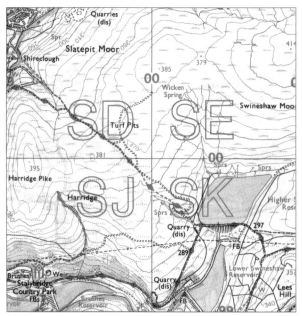

Look in the map key to find out which of the two large squares you're in. Figure 3.4a shows it could be either SJ, SK, SD or SE. A glance to the top corner of the map sheet shows the letters SK (Figure 3.4b). Check this on a map for yourself. The map extract in Figure 3.3 lies in the segment of the map covered by the SK squares. It's then back to Figure 3.3. To read the number part of a grid reference simply draw a capital L around the nearest grid lines. The numbers of the vertical line are read first followed by the horizontal line. So the four-figure grid reference for the footpath junction in Figure 3.3 is SK 06 90.

This grid reference is relevant not only for the path junction A, but for wherever you are in that square, so junction B has the same four-figure grid reference. To be able to differentiate between A and B you need to further subdivide the square as shown in Figure 3.5a. Again draw a capital L around the nearest grid lines and read the new reference: vertical first, then horizontal. The six-figure reference for junction A is now SK 063 902, and for B is SK 061 904.

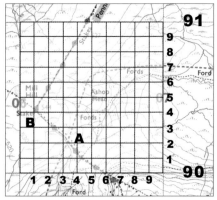

Figure 3.5a

A single grid square subdivided to obtain an six-figure grid reference

A four-figure grid reference describes an area of 1km² (or 1,000,000 m²) and a six-figure brings this down to 10,000m². It is possible using the Romer scale found on some compasses to get your grid reference up to an eight-figure (100m²) level of accuracy. (The eight-figure reference for A is SK 0633 9022.) (See Figure 3.5b.)

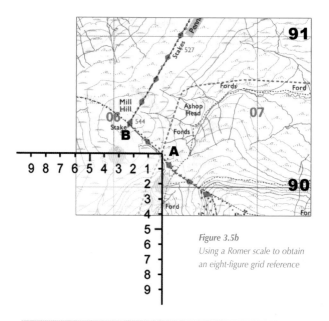

Figure 3.5b
Using a Romer scale to obtain
an eight-figure grid reference

GPSs regularly report grid references to eight- or, in some cases, 10-figure accuracy, but have only recently (with the establishment of the WAAS ground stations) become accurate to that degree. If you're using your GPS to fix your location on a map you only need to use the first three figures from each half of the grid reference (to give a six-figure reference). A GPS reference may appear as SK 12345 65432, SK 12345 E 65432 N or even SK E12345 N65432: use SK 123 654 as your reference. This will be enough to relocate yourself and make an accurate bearing to your next feature (see Chapter 4). (**Note** The 'E' and 'N' above refer to the terms 'eastings' and 'northings'; eastings refer to the grid numbers along the top and bottom of your map, and northings to those up the side.)

Setting the map

Have you ever set off on a walk and turned in the wrong direction right at the start? Or taken a footpath on the right instead of the left? I certainly have – and I know I'm not alone! It's easy to do – you want to start walking and so only give the map a cursory glance before setting off.

The sure-fire way of preventing this is to 'set' or orientate your map – to turn it round so that the features on the map coincide with how they appear on the ground. In other words if you're walking from north to south turn the map upside down. You can set a map in two ways: first by lining up a linear feature on the map, like a road or a stream, with the run of it on the ground. The second, easier way is to use your compass. Remember that the red end of the needle points north, so with your compass on your map rotate the map until the red end of the needle is pointing to the top (north) of the map (see Figures 3.6a & b). Now if you know you want to turn in a certain direction on your map at the start of your walk, turn in the same direction on the ground.

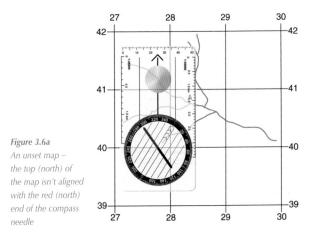

Figure 3.6a

*An unset map –
the top (north) of
the map isn't aligned
with the red (north)
end of the compass
needle*

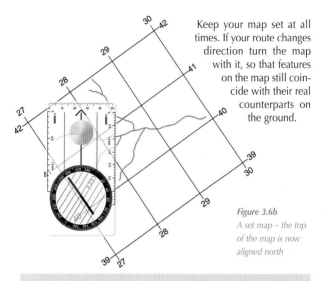

Keep your map set at all times. If your route changes direction turn the map with it, so that features on the map still coincide with their real counterparts on the ground.

Figure 3.6b
A set map – the top of the map is now aligned north

GPSs sometimes give you the option of having the map screen display in a variety of ways, for example with north always at the top, or with your direction always at the top. The latter is the equivalent of you setting the map. Obviously if you're not moving the screen direction information is not necessarily accurate, but it will correct itself quickly once you start walking again. My advice would be to set your device preferences so that your direction is always at the top, especially if your GPS can display a map.

The map key

A map is a graphical representation of what we can see on the ground, and the map makers use certain conventions to represent common features – the key. Understanding the key is an essential part of map reading, and despite what we may remember from our geography lessons of yesteryear it's not that hard. Start by taking your map out on walks you do often. Keep comparing the map with the ground and see how paths, walls, fences, hedges, streams and so on are represented. By comparing reality with the map you'll quickly build up an understanding of the main symbols. When you next walk in a new area you'll need only occasionally to refer to the map's key to check out new features.

It is important to understand the symbols for public rights of way. Figure 3.7 shows how these are represented on a 1:25,000 OS map alongside the way that a path (that is not necessarily a right of way) is shown.

··················	Path
– – – – – – –	Footpath
—— —— ——	Bridleway
+++++++++	Byway open to all traffic
–·–·–·–·–	Road used as a public path (From late 2004 roads used as public paths are to be redesignated as 'Restricted byways'. Restricted byways provide a right of way for walkers, horse riders, cyclists and other non-mechanically propelled vehicles)

Public rights of way shown on this map have been taken from local authority definitive maps and later amendments. The map includes changes notified to Ordnance Survey by 1st Sep 2005. Rights of way are liable to change and may not be clearly defined on the ground. Please check with the relevant local authority for the latest information

The representation on this map of any other road, track or path is no evidence of the existence of a right of way

● ● ●	Other routes with public access (not normally shown in urban areas)

The exact nature of the rights on these routes and the existence of any restrictions may be checked with the local highway authority. Alignments are based on the best information available

◆ ◆	National Trail / Long Distance Route ; Recreational Route
– – – – – – –	Permitted footpath } Footpaths and bridleways along which landowners have permitted public use but which are not rights of way. The agreement may be withdrawn
—— —— ——	Permitted bridleway
● ● ●	Traffic-free cycle route
[1]	National cycle network route number - traffic free
■1	National cycle network route number - on road

Figure 3.7 Symbols for paths and rights of way

When the OS mark a path or a track on the map, they are marking anything that is visible on the ground whether it's been made by a herd of cows on their twice-daily trip to the milking sheds or by walkers on a public footpath. The OS don't know whether that path or track is a public right of way or not. It is up to the various Highway Authorities (usually the County and Metropolitan Councils) to mark on the public rights of way (ROW): the green symbols found on an OS map. Figure 3.8 shows a map extract with a variety of paths, tracks and rights of way.

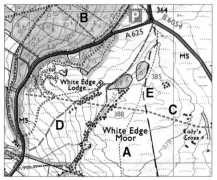

Figure 3.8
Map extract showing all sorts of paths, tracks and rights of way

Route A A visible path, but without the green ROW symbols, so not a public right of way.

Route B Look carefully and you'll notice the short black path symbols underneath the green ROW footpath symbols. This is a public foot-path that is visible on the ground.

Route C A public right of way (a footpath) which isn't visible on the ground (there are no black dashes beneath the green).

Route D The longer green dashes denote a bridleway, but the absence of black dashes shows that the route cannot be seen on the ground. However, follow the route up past White Edge Lodge and you'll notice that it becomes visible on the ground.

Route E Not a route at all; the longer black dashes do not represent a path but a boundary (in this case the boundary of a Unitary authority, Sheffield City Council). By the words 'White Edge Moor' the boundary runs alongside a wall.

Note the colour of the map on the majority of this extract. It has a pale brown tinge all over apart from the bottom left corner and a small section up the left-hand side. This represents access land which gives you the right to walk anywhere (with a few restrictions: see below). You can not only walk along the non-ROW paths shown on this map extract, you can also wander off path. Figure 3.9 shows how the OS represent access land on a 1:25000 map.

Figure 3.9
Map extract showing access land

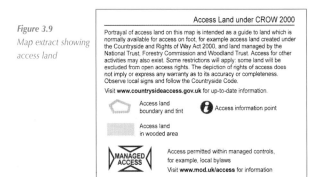

Access Land under CROW 2000

Portrayal of access land on this map is intended as a guide to land which is normally available for access on foot, for example access land created under the Countryside and Rights of Way Act 2000, and land managed by the National Trust, Forestry Commission and Woodland Trust. Access for other activities may also exist. Some restrictions will apply: some land will be excluded from open access rights. The depiction of rights of access does not imply or express any warranty as to its accuracy or completeness. Observe local signs and follow the Countryside Code.

Visit **www.countrysideaccess.gov.uk** for up-to-date information.

⬠ Access land boundary and tint   ⓘ Access information point

▨ Access land in wooded area

⬖MANAGED ACCESS⬗   Access permitted within managed controls, for example, local bylaws
Visit **www.mod.uk/access** for information

Navigating by GPS can feel like a liberating experience as you are freed from the paper map and detailed compass work of traditional navigaton. Now you can head from location to location following the screen directions. It is important, however, that you refer to the map to check that you are walking where you should. GPSs cannot interpret bends and wiggles in rights of way, nor whether where you are walking is on a right of way or in access land. Your unit will tell you how to get to a feature in a straight line. However, rights of way are rarely straight, and if you're not in access land you must stick to the footpaths. (If you're in access land you can walk in a straight line regardless of paths on the ground.)

Figure 3.10 A short GPS route showing the limita-tions of following the on-screen route exactly

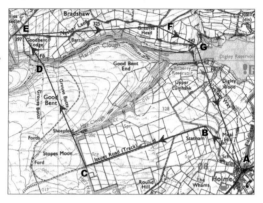

Take the route shown in Figure 3.10. You've entered the route A–G and back to A in your GPS as a series of waypoints. If you follow the GPS's instruction to the letter your route A–B would not follow the green dotted 'route with other public access'. The route B–C is fine; a straight-line path will be echoed by the GPS instructions. From C–D the GPS will follow the red line shown in Figure 3.10 but the path (a visible route, as denoted by the black dashes that lie under the ROW green dashes) obviously follows a different line. However this section of the walk is in access land (shown by the pale brown shading) which means you aren't obliged to stick to rights of way and can walk where you like (restrictions may sometimes apply, for example the access land may be closed during the game shooting season or in times of high fire risk – this does not, however, affect your rights on a public footpath). The GPS route also crosses the valley of Hey Clough, which involves nego-tiating a steep drop and some rock outcrops. The right of way follows the easier route round the head of the valley: a prime example of why you should always look at the route on the map rather than follow the GPS directions religiously.

At point D you'll probably want to cross the river at the footbridge so using your GPS – or map skills – to get you there is sensible. The route D–E starts in access land and ends at the right-angled turn in the footpath outside the access land. To get there you are probably advised to follow the path on the ground rather than try to follow the straight-line route indicated by your GPS. Likewise E–F and F–G (all outside access land): following the on-screen directions will lead you into trouble. Not only will you not find any stiles or gates along your route but you are not following the right of way so are likely to upset the local landowner. The final section G–A would include a swim across the reservoir if you followed the on-screen directions, as well as tres-passing across private fields.

Contours

Understanding contours is perhaps one of the most difficult aspects of map reading. Not so much what they are, but what they represent on the ground. Valleys are usually straightforward to spot, especially the deeper ones – the Vs made by the contour lines always point upstream – but what about spurs, ridges, escarpments or saddles?

The old-fashioned (but still effective) way of learning about contours is to go out and experience them. Allow time on your walk to sit and stare and match the shape of the ground with the way it is represented on the map. Look at a section you're about to encounter on a walk and study the contours carefully – will you be heading uphill? If so how steep is the path (the closer the contours the steeper the ground)? The more you do this the better you'll become at inter-preting contour patterns.

The hi-tech approach is to launch your digital mapping software and use the 3D feature. Find an interesting looking area on the map, and study the contour patterns. Work out what you're looking at, then press the 3D option and see if you're right. You can adjust the vertical distortion to accentuate or reduce the vertical scale and move around the feature to study its shape from all sides (see Chapter 7).

Figures 3.11 1a–5b 'Flat' map extracts with their 3D counterparts
(3D images courtesy of Tracklogs Digital Mapping Software)

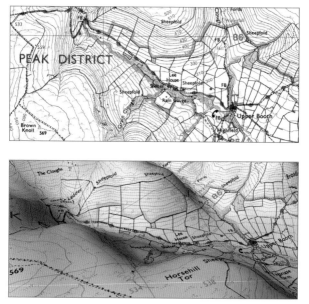

Figures 3.11 1a & b

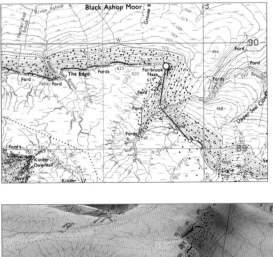

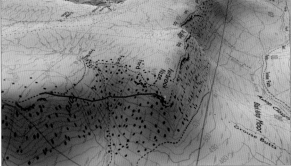

Figures 3.11 2a & b

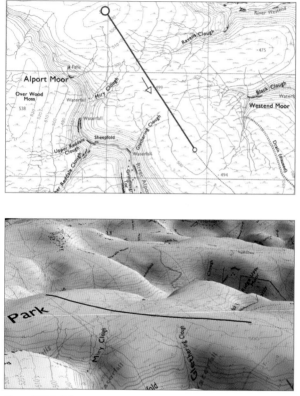

Figures 3.11 3a & b

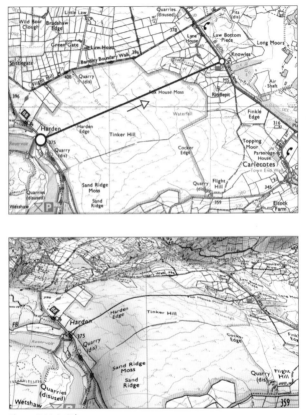

Figures 3.11 4a & b

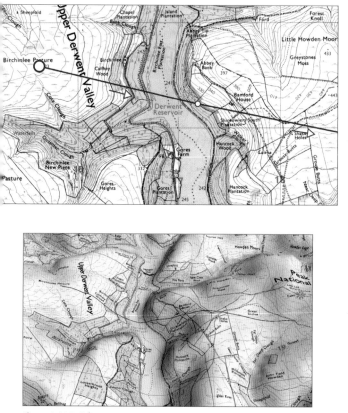

Figures 3.11 5a & b

Understanding contours is important for the GPS user. No one has yet invented a GPS that interprets the shape of the ground, so all distances and bearings are given assuming the landscape is flat. For example: you're halfway around a walk on the moors and decide you need to head back to your starting point. You key in its location and start to walk. If you haven't referred to the map, you'd presumably follow the direction indicated by the GPS. If you had looked at the map you might notice that the direct route drops you off a cliff into a deep valley and up the other side en route for your car. Careful map study would reveal a better route than the direct option.

Figure 3.12 shows an example in 2D and 3D. You are at point A and decide, for whatever reason, not to continue your route. You find the waypoint for the end of the footpath at B in your GPS and follow the direct route indicated by the red line. As you can see in Figure 3.12b, the route drops down into a steep valley, up the other side and over the moor before heading through the pine plantation to arrive at point B. A look at your map (once you had identified your location) would reveal a far better option. Enter the grid reference of the shooting cabin (C) and follow the GPS until you reach it. You're then on a relatively level path that leads you round to the Roman road and the roadside. It might be a longer walk, but will be considerably easier and quicker.

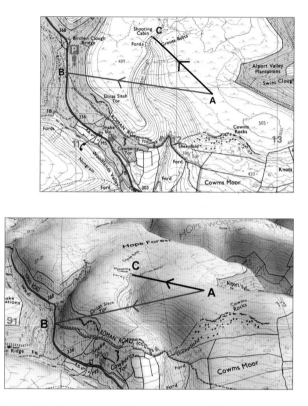

Figures 3.12a & b Map extract and 3D version showing a GPS bearing back to the start of a walk across a deep valley (3D image courtesy of Tracklogs Digital Mapping Software)

Planning ahead

One important map skill to develop is the ability to plan ahead. At the start of each stage of your walk study the route carefully. What features will you see along the way? Is the ground rising or falling, and how steeply? Commit these to memory and mentally tick off the information as you progress. If what you experience doesn't match what you expected then you are either walking in the wrong direction or have interpreted the map incorrectly. A well-developed map memory will reduce your reliance on the map too. You can study it, put it down and enjoy each stage of the walk before moving on to ther next one.

If you use your GPS to navigate don't forget to use the map too – it's easy to do. I make no apology for reiterating this important point! You might be following your GPS on a bearing to your next location. Make sure you check where this is on the map and study the features and contour shapes you'll see along the way. When you're following your GPS you can then check it's sending you in the right direction.

The compass

A GPS isn't a compass. Some have an electronic compass as an added feature, but this is not as flexible as a conventional compass. Even if you intend to spend the day navigating with your GPS, always carry a compass in your rucksack as well. If your GPS fails you have a back-up system which won't let you down – assuming you know how to use it.

Figure 3.13 shows a basic compass similar to that used on the hills by thousands of walkers: it has all the essential bits without the extras.

The most important part is the needle. The red end points north and the other end points south (assuming the compass is not close to a magnetic source – check the effect of your walking equipment on a

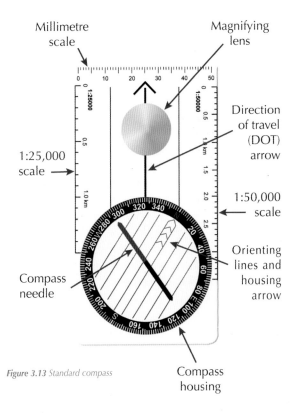

Millimetre scale

Magnifying lens

Direction of travel (DOT) arrow

1:25,000 scale →

1:50,000 ← scale

Orienting lines and housing arrow

Compass needle

Compass housing

Figure 3.13 Standard compass

compass. Does the needle deflect when you bring it close to your camera, watch or GPS for example?).

The needle is contained within the compass housing which should be marked into the 360° of a circle, in 2° divisions maximum, along with the cardinal points N, S, E and W. Anything greater than this means you won't be able to read a bearing accurately enough. The compass housing should rotate easily, but not so freely that you could knock it accidentally. The housing arrow is printed on the base of the housing (pointing to the N on the edge of the housing) plus a series of parallel lines known as the orienting lines.

The housing is contained within a base plate on which – on a good compass – other features appear such as the Direction of Travel (DOT) arrow: the arrow which indicates the direction you need to travel in. The magnifying lens is an optional extra, but my guess is that if you don't need it now to help spot fine details on the map, you will as the years progress. The scales and millimetre ruler help you calculate distances and will also come in useful.

That's it. Such a compass should cost around £15. Avoid compasses that are as cheap as chips. There are many differences between a cheap and nasty compass and a good one. Build quality will be obvious, but one of the unseen differences is the addition of an antistatic substance to the fluid inside the housing in a good compass. The cheapies don't have this, which might result in your needle pointing in the wrong direction if it picks up a static charge in your fleece pocket.

What is a bearing?

A bearing is simply the angle between N(orth), where you are (A) and where you wish to go (B) (Figure 3.14) To take a bearing on a map requires three simple steps.

Figures 3.15a–c show a simple map with point A being where you are and point B being where

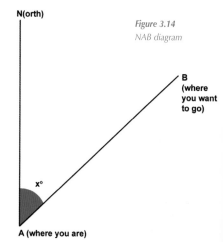

Figure 3.14
NAB diagram

B (where you want to go)

x°

A (where you are)

N(orth)

you wish to go. (Always use the feature, not the name, as the point you read a bearing from and to: for example point B may be called Borrowdale Rocks. These words will be the equivalent of 300m long on the map. The feature, not the name, will be in the correct location!)

1 Place the edge of the compass carefully so it goes through features A and B, making sure the DOT arrow is pointing in the direction you wish to go (towards B). (Figure 3.15a)
2 Turn the compass housing so the housing arrow points north on the map and the orienting lines are parallel to the vertical grid lines. (Figure 3.15b)
3 Take the compass off the map and read the bearing off against the DOT arrow (the DOT line may extend under the compass housing to aid accurate reading). (Figure 3.15c)

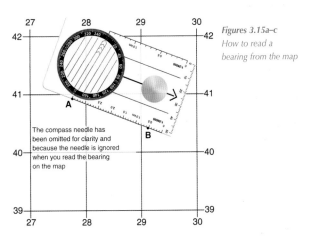

The compass needle has been omitted for clarity and because the needle is ignored when you read the bearing on the map

Figures 3.15a–c
How to read a bearing from the map

Figure 3.15a

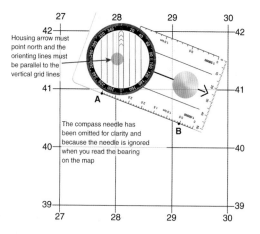

Housing arrow must point north and the orienting lines must be parallel to the vertical grid lines

The compass needle has been omitted for clarity and because the needle is ignored when you read the bearing on the map

Figure 3.15b

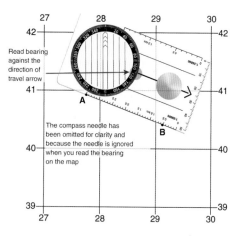

Read bearing against the direction of travel arrow

The compass needle has been omitted for clarity and because the needle is ignored when you read the bearing on the map

Figure 3.15c

> **Note** In Figure 3.15 the compass needle has been omitted for clarity, but also for a more important reason. Apart from when you are setting the map with a compass (page 26), always ignore the needle when the compass is lying on the map.

So now you have a bearing: the angle between north, where you are and where you wish to go. In order to walk on this bearing you need to make an adjustment to allow for the difference between the map's north and the compass's north: the magnetic variation (MV).

The grid network on your map I talked about earlier is drawn so the vertical lines all meet at a point in infinity called **grid north**. Your compass needle, being magnetic, points to **magnetic north**. The difference between the two is the **magnetic variation**.

To make life more exciting magnetic north is constantly moving; it is currently somewhere in northeastern Canada and moving slowly east. Assuming you are reading this somewhere in the UK sometime before AD2025, magnetic north is west of grid north.

Figure 3.16 shows a simple picture of the situation. Notice how your

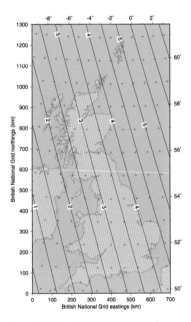

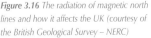

Figure 3.16 The radiation of magnetic north lines and how it affects the UK (courtesy of the British Geological Survey – NERC)

location in the UK will affect the degree of MV. Taking into account the fact that magnetic north is moving east by half a degree every three years (roughly), you need to make sure you are up-to-date with the current MV.

There are two ways to do this. The first is to look at the key of a current OS map, where you'll find two sentences under the section headed 'North Points'. Ignore the first (which relates to the difference between true – polar – north and grid north); it's the second sentence which is important. The 2007 Explorer OL24 White Peak map has the following:

(For the East and West sheets)... magnetic north is estimated at 3°14' and 3°07' west of grid north respectively for July 2007.

You won't be able to adjust your compass housing by less than half a degree, so round the figure off to the nearest ½° (30'). (In 2007 I'm using a MV of 3° in the Peak District.) So to alter your compass bearing to make it a magnetic bearing instead of a grid bearing remember this little ditty.

From Grid to Mag add, from Mag to Grid get rid.

This ditty works in the UK and anywhere magnetic north is west of grid north, so to convert your grid bearing to a magnetic one (grid to mag) you need to add the MV. So if we're assuming the MV is 3° and the bearing in example Figure 3.15 was 109°, the magnetic bearing is 112° for 2007. Turn your compass around 3° so it now reads 112°.

The second way to find out the MV is to visit **www.nearby.org.uk**. Enter your grid reference (or postcode), press return, then scroll down to the link 'Magnetic Variation' and follow the instructions.

Holding your compass

Figure 3.17 shows how you should hold your compass: a conventional base plate compass (3.17a) and a sighting compass (3.17b). To line up the compass for walking turn it so the red end of the needle

Figures 3.17a & b
Holding a compass

Figure 3.17a *(left)*
Figure 3.17b *(below)*

Figure 3.18
Walk in the
direction indi-
cated by the
DOT arrow

lines up with the housing arrow. Note in Figure 3.17a how the arms are locked into the body; this helps prevent you twisting your wrists to line up your needle and housing arrow – move your whole body. Walk in the direction indicated by the DOT arrow (Figure 3.18). As you turn the compass your body will also turn, so your toes, nose and DOT arrow will be pointing in the same direction. You are now almost ready to proceed.

> **Note** Be careful when holding your compass that it is not close to other magnetic objects such as watches or cameras – and your GPS. If your needle is affected by something you are carrying you may need to hold your compass further away from you.

Walking on a bearing

Let's run over what a bearing is again: the angle between north, where you are and where you want to go. If that bearing was drawn on the ground we would have two lines, one pointing to north (now magnetic north (A–N) and one to where you are heading (A–B) (Figure 3.19). Your task when following a bearing is to walk along

Figure 3.19 NAB on the ground

the line leading to where you are heading (A–B). If that line existed on the ground, things would be simple. Instead you need to imagine that line on the ground and pick physical features along it to walk to, until you reach your final destination. I do this by concentrating on the central pivot point of the needle, then gently raising my head to look along the direction of travel and extending it out across the landscape (Figure 3.20).

Figure 3.20 The bearing extended out from the DOT line

Such features could be a large boulder or a tree, or a small patch of distinctive vegetation. How far ahead the feature is will depend on a number of factors, but you need to ensure that you will be able to identify it as you get closer. A prominent lump of heather can blend in with its neighbours very easily as you walk towards it. If there is absolutely nothing to spot, or the hill is shrouded in mist, you could use one of your walking companions as the marker. Send him off in the right direction (not too far – you need to be able to communicate with him!) line him up with the imaginary line, and then walk towards him. Repeat this process until you get to your destination.

This technique is called leapfrogging, and is a superb method for accurate compass work.

Note It takes twice as long to walk the section as you are in effect walking it twice. If you have to spend any time leapfrogging on your walk, it will seriously affect the the overall timing.

Back bearings

Being able to check you are heading in the right direction is important, and pretty simple to do. You know the red end of your compass needle points north. The other end must therefore point south.

When you wish to walk on a bearing line up the red end of the needle and the housing arrow and walk in the direction indicated by the DOT arrow.

To do a back bearing line up the other end of the needle with the housing arrow and look back along the DOT arrow (Figure 3.21). This should be pointing back to your departure point – if it isn't, realign yourself. If you're leapfrogging the person out front can use back bearings to check the accuracy of the back marker – a useful double check.

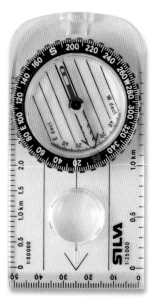

Figure 3.21
Back bearing on the compass

Note This technique should only be used when you are in view of your original departure point. Once this is out of sight a back bearing isn't worth doing.

Timing and pacing

Every walker should know how long a particular section of a walk is going to take, and how far he has advanced along it. Timing, they say, is everything, and the walking world has it's own timing master in the form of a Victorian gentleman called Naismith. He devised a formula to calculate how long a walk or section would take. Translated into metric it reads as follows.

4km an hour plus 1 minute for every 10m climbed.

Having worked with groups for 20+ years I find this formula works well. However, if I'm on my own I walk faster; if I'm out with a young family, much slower. You need to adapt this formula to suit your needs. If you walk at 5kph use that in your calculations. If you are a slower walker adjust it accordingly. Likewise consider additional time for climbing. If you dislike descents and take them very cautiously add in an adjustment for those too.

Once you have arrived at a formula that works for you, use it to time shorter sections. A speed of 4kph breaks down to 15 minutes per km and 1.5 minutes for 100m. So if you've got 400m to walk with a 30m ascent, it's going to take you around 9 minutes to walk it (4 x 1.5 minutes = 6 minutes + 3 x 1 minute = 9 minutes). It's not an exact science – as the ninth minute ticks round you probably won't stumble over your destination – but you will be in the vicinity. Being aware of how long a section will take will prevent you from over-shooting the point you are looking for, a trap some walkers fall into when walking on a bearing.

Pacing is another habit that's worth developing. Find somewhere you can measure out 100m (a running track is ideal). Walk the distance a few times, counting how many paces you take to cover 100m. I tend to count in double paces to make things easier (a double pace is every time my, say, left foot hits the ground – see Figure 3.22).

One double pace

Figure 3.22 Double pacing

So perhaps you're up on the moors and want to be certain that you'll hit a footpath to take you off the hill, and which you've meas-ured on your map to be 300m away. Pace out the distance and you'll arrive at your descent path. Once again you're more likely to be in the vicinity of the path rather than right at the junction, but you shouldn't be too far away.

Of course walking on a flat, well-maintained surface is easier than striding over knee-deep heather, so try measuring your paces over a variety of oft-walked terrain and see how much they vary.

Practical exercise

As can be seen in this quick overview there is no substitute for good map and compass skills. Read this book's sister title *Navigation: Techniques and skills for walkers* (Cicerone Press) for a more comprehensive overview, and consider attending a navigation course to gain some vital practice in controlled conditions (**www.navigationcourses.co.uk**).

Try to put some of the theory you've just read about into practice. You need to reach the stage where you can rely on your map and compass skills; this is vital if the conditions are poor and your GPS suffers a rare problem. It might not happen often, but you must be prepared for when it does.

CHAPTER 4

Basic Navigation with a GPS

This book is not an A–Z to using your particular make of GPS; they all come with a user guide, and usually a quick start guide too. This should be sufficient to get you navigating round the various screens and menus. I am therefore assuming you have had a good play with your GPS and have set it up for your time zone and grid system, and allowed it to get a fix on your location. This chapter will build on your current knowledge and get you using it properly.

How are you planning to navigate?

How do you navigate yourself round a walk? Do you follow a route from a guidebook or a magazine? Do you photocopy the route (or carry the whole publication), using the sketch map or OS map extract as your sole mapping source? (Hopefully not: all walkers should carry a proper map of the area. What would happen if you strayed off the printed route and therefore off the sketch map?) Do you plan your route assiduously beforehand (possibly using a guidebook as inspiration), filling in a route card or marking your map in some way before you embark on your walk? Or are you a free spirit who decides where to walk on the day?

    These three scenarios can all benefit from using a GPS. The guidebook follower can leave his GPS running to record the route; when he starts to wonder where he is he can use the GPS to relocate himself. The route planner can use the GPS alongside digital mapping software to enhance the planning process and transfer the route to the GPS; the free spirit can continue to enjoy his random wanderings, safe in the knowledge that he can relocate himself at any stage of the walk. He can also enter a grid reference as a waypoint should he wish to go to a certain location. We'll explore these techniques in more detail later.

Where am I?

Stop any GPS user on the hill and ask them how they use their unit. The chances are pretty high you'll get a response along the lines of 'Oh I only switch it on when I want to know where I am.' So let's deal with this first.

Switch on your unit and wait! If you've not had it on for a while it may take a time for the GPS to find and identify the satellites and in turn feed you a location. What that location tells you will depend on how you've set up your GPS.

As described in Chapter 3, the UK is covered by a grid system designed to overcome the problems caused by the fact that the earth is a globe and wobbles on its north–south axis from time to time. This artificial grid is known as the OSGB36. Unless you're a lover of latitude and longitude (and assuming you are in Great Britain), you should ensure your GPS is set to show your location in OSGB or British Grid depending on its make or model. If you're in Northern or Southern Ireland you'll need to set your GPS to the Irish Grid.

The location will look something like SK 24345 62787, or maybe SK 24345 N62787 or SK 24345 E 62787 N. In Chapter 3 we covered what these grid letters refer to, but let's consider the numbers and what the GPS is telling us. You'll recall that a four-figure grid reference (SK 24 62 using the above example) is only accurate to within a square kilometre, and a six-figure grid

Figure 4.1 GPS screen... where am I?

reference (SK 243 627) brings us in to an area of 100 x 100m. Adding another digit gets us down to 10 x 10m, and finally the 10-figure reference above is accurate to within 1m.

On the face of it this seems fantastic: we can locate ourselves to within 1m. However, consider this statement on the Ordnance Survey's website:

> Positional accuracy with a single receiver to civilian users approximately equals 5m to 10m, 95 percent of the time, and the height accuracy is generally 15m to 20m, 95 percent of the time.

Even though your GPS is giving a position to within 1m, most of the time it's 5–10m out. This is pretty good, but let's consider what even 10m accuracy means on a 1:25,000 map. As we saw in Chapter 3, 1km on the ground is represented by 4cm on the map. This means that 1cm is 250m, 4mm is 100m, and 0.4mm on a map is equivalent to 10m on the ground (an almost impossible distance to measure on the map unless you are at a discrete point such as a stream or wall junction). If 0.4mm is impossible a 10-figure grid reference with 1m accuracy is represented by 0.04mm on the map. Don't even bother!

Some GPSs give the option of selecting how detailed your grid reference should be. A six-figure reference is adequate, but there's no need to bother with anything greater than eight.

Once you have this figure, what are you going to do with it? Presumably you switched on your GPS because you weren't sure where you were in the first place, so once you have your grid reference apply it back to your map.

As Figure 4.2 illustrates GPSs with OS mapping on board are fine to an extent, but you should always refer the location to a paper map as you get a broader overview of your location. But what next? Did the information surprise you? If you have drifted off your planned route, you'll now need to relocate yourself by working out where you want to be and entering that location as a new waypoint.

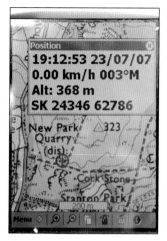

Figure 4.2 GPS screen and location on map; note that the altitude is given as 368m but you are actually at 315m (see Chapter 2)

Practical exercise
On a short route walk to a feature, identify your grid reference from the GPS. Check it concurs with the feature's grid reference on the map. Use the Romer on the navigation aid supplied with this book to get an eight-figure grid reference.

Entering a new location

It might sound obvious, but in order to enter a new location you first need to know where you want to go. Even if your GPS has an OS map on-screen, you're still better referring to the map and calculating a grid reference.

Once you have the grid reference, enter the details into your GPS, select the Go To option and follow the on-screen instructions.

Different GPS receivers require you to go through different steps to enter a new location. My Lowrance iFinder gives me a number of different ways of entering a new location, but I have to edit an existing waymark on my Magellan eXplorist.

Practical exercise
Ensure you know how to enter a new location into your GPS
quickly and effectively. Your manual will give you some indication of how to do this, but remember you may be working in poor
conditions where speed and accuracy is vital. Identify a number
of grid references on a map and enter the details into your GPS.
Remember to give each point a unique identifying name you can
recognise later.

Getting off-route – and getting back again

The above steps are fine if you aren't far off-route. However, if you
are way off-route then a straight-line route back to your desired location may not be feasible or even safe. A careful study of the map will
show you the best options. Figure 4.3 illustrates this point. You have
come off the summit of Bleaklow too far south and find yourself at
point A, The Pike. However, you need to be over the other side of
Yellowslacks Brook at Dog Rock. Entering the coordinates for Dog

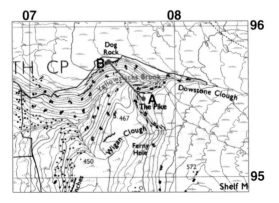

Figure 4.3 The Go To option can give an unsuitable route

Rock into the GPS and activating the Go To option will result in you being sent on the direct route indicated by the red line. If you were to head off on the route without referring to the map you'd end up dropping over 80m via a series of crags to the valley floor before an 80m climb out the other side.

The preferable route would be to work your way around the head of the valley as indicated by Figure 4.4. Points C, D and E are all made-up, but were chosen to ensure that the route taken doesn't drop too far in altitude and that the river is crossed at a point where the wall or fence that runs round the north side of the brook is avoided. Enter the coordinates for the new points into the GPS as new waymark points. Then use the Go To function to navigate from one to the next until you get round to Dog Rock.

Remember If you enter an eight-figure grid reference into a GPS set up for a 10-figure one, put a 0 in the 5th and 10th positions (SK 07550 E 95760 N).

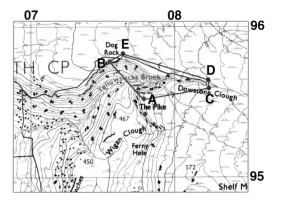

Figure 4.4 Work out a better route by referring to the map

Point	Grid reference
A	07800 95500
B	07550 95760
C	08240 95580
D	08230 95660
E	07640 95800

If you are navigating your way round a deep valley as above, accurate grid references aren't that important. However, you may find it useful to use the scale or Romer on your compass to take a more accurate reference.

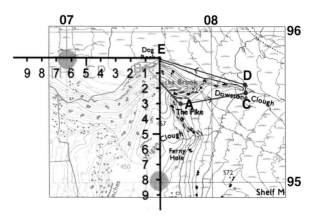

Figure 4.5 Using a Romer on the above map extract

Practical exercise

Take a map for a hilly area with which you're familiar. Select a few deep valleys and try to identify a sensible route round the head of each. Are you using features marked on the map, or are you having to use made-up points?

To help with your confidence in choosing these points, take an area of ground you can wander round freely (it doesn't have to be a large expanse, but big enough to be able to identify separate grid references). Make a few light pencil marks on the map away from any features. Enter their grid references into your GPS and navigate from one to the next, eventually returning to the starting point. Did you get round OK?

Using your GPS with a map

The above example illustrates why solely using a GPS is not a good idea. **Always use it in conjunction with a map**. This will ensure you always have an overview of where you are within the wider landscape. Keep referring to the surrounding hills and other major landscape features (invaluable should the GPS fail on you totally or start giving inaccurate readings). Never believe a grid reference without checking it fits with the information on the map and on the ground. It's very easy to believe technology, especially as it gives us answers so easily!

Creating a route

The steps you went through to negotiate around the valley in the above example is the first step towards creating a route. Most walkers will think about the route in advance, even if only to work out where to park the car, and in which direction to leave the car park. Plotting your route into your GPS before you start would seem like a sensible way of using it.

The other more free-form way of route planning is to do it on the fly, and there's a whole host of reasons why you might want to do this. Perhaps you're a wanderer who makes decisions about where to go as the spirit takes you; maybe you planned a route that you want to extend; the weather might have changed for the worse and you decide to curtail your previously planned route to get off the hill sooner. Whatever the reasons and location the steps are identical.

1 First decide where you want to go. Study the map carefully and choose a suitable route that fulfils your aims.
2 Break down the route into suitable legs or sections.
3 Note the grid reference for the start of each section and your end point.
4 Enter each grid reference as a waypoint in your GPS, giving each point a suitable name or consecutive number (names are preferable).
5 Enter the New Route section of your GPS and enter the waypoints in the order you wish to walk them.
6 Save the route and give it a suitable name.
7 Check your waypoints again in case you entered any points incorrectly. Edit any if necessary.

Entering a new route on the go is a time-consuming process. You have to enter the grid reference and give the location a meaningful name (at the very least). If you have to make a comprehensive readjustment to your route you're in for quite a delay to your walk. If you're with a small group of mates who are happy to wait that's fine, but if you're in charge of a bunch of less experienced walkers who are relying on your navigation and leadership skills then you're going to have a disgruntled group to deal with. Alternative or emergency routes are discussed in Chapter 5.

The first three steps above are the initial steps of constructing a paper route card (see Figure 5.4, Chapter 5). Along with the height climbed, the horizontal distance for each section and an estimation of the time it'll take to walk, the route card provides a very useful summary of a day's walk.

Navigating a route

You've entered your planned route – now you have to follow it! Most GPS units have a few different screens that will guide you around your route. Most walkers will probably use the Map screen, which shows the track to take and will also trace your walked route. The other possibility is the Track or Navigation screen which will show you graphically and in figures your bearing or track. Your GPS may also have an electronic compass which will show the direction in which to head to arrive at your intended location. Which screen you use is determined by what's available on your GPS and personal preference.

Figures 4.6a–c A variety of screens showing how routes can be followed

Figure 4.6b

Figure 4.6c

You can also choose how to follow your GPS on the ground:

1 Continuously referring to the screen and following the route 'exactly'.
2 Occasionally referring to the screen and walking in a broad direction.

1 Continuous reference

Once you have entered your route, the GPS will give you the directions to the next waypoint. By continuously referring to the screen try to keep on the desired course until you reach it. It doesn't matter if you wander slightly off course as you'll be redirected until you are back on route.

Remember the GPS is trying to work to an accuracy of 1m, but the grid reference you'll have taken off the map will only be accurate up to 10m at best. Keep in mind what you're heading for, so that when you get close to the destination you can spot it on the ground.

2 Using your GPS to give you a broad direction

Your GPS will indicate the direction you need to head in. Look ahead in this direction (similar to how you would look along the DOT arrow of a compass) and identify a feature broadly in the direction you're heading. Walk to this object (you don't need to keep an eye on your GPS continuously; pop it in a pocket or just hold it in your hand). When you've arrived at your feature, repeat the process until you reach your desired location.

Your destination will presumably be an identifiable feature, like a stream junction, or meeting point of two walls or a large rock outcrop. As in the previous example, remember what you're looking for and don't rely on your GPS to guide you in exactly to the point. Use your eyes and common sense.

If you're following a compass bearing and wander off course you may be in danger of missing your intended target especially if you are navigating in bad weather. Using a GPS avoids this possibility. The GPS will continually update your position and alter the information on screen to get you to the desired location.

However, be careful how your GPS tells you that you have reached your location. Many will tell you that you've got there before you

Figure 4.7 Arrival alarm on the Lowrance
Expedition C GPS

actually have and, if you're following a route, will want to send you to your next location automatically. One GPS I used recently moved me on to my next location 100m short of my destination. That's fine in theory, but I like to walk to known features and viewpoints. My GPS was preventing me from doing so unless I remained on the ball and continued onto my viewpoint manually. On investigation in the set-up menu I discovered I could adjust the 'accuracy' of the arrival alarm which I have subsequently done down to 10m.

Before we progress, let's consider these two very different methods. The first demands your constant attention on the GPS; the second requires occasional reference plus a regard for your surroundings and destination.

The 'continuous reference method' can result in you divorcing yourself from the landscape through which you are walking. You'll become much more concerned with following the on-screen route and less concerned with where you are. Good navigation is about being aware of where you are within a landscape and less concerned with your exact location at any particular moment. Staring at the GPS screen will mean you take your attention off the bigger picture. On a more prosaic level, if your attention is on the screen you won't notice where you're putting your feet and will end up flat on your face very quickly – I've done it!

The second method avoids these problems. You're spotting a broad direction and can then concentrate on finding the best route to get to your intended destination. And you can enjoy the views, have a conversation with your friends and have that valuable thinking time that many of us enjoy when walking. Only when you're drawing nearer to your destination do you have to concentrate more closely on your navigation

I use my GPS when teaching groups to navigate with map and compass. I set them a destination for a particular route, enter the location into my GPS and set off with them. I can then wander about the moors concentrating on the group and their needs rather than worrying about the direction in which I'm walking. I know the GPS will get me back on track if necessary.

Practical exercise

1 Plan a route. Enter the waypoints into your GPS, giving each a sensible name or at least a sequential number. Then head for the hills! At your starting point find the first waypoint, tell your GPS to Go To it, and set off. Once there, head for the next waypoint and so on, until you've completed your first GPS walk. Don't forget your map and continually refer back to it, so you know precisely where you are. Don't forget to analyse the walk at the end. Was it successful? Did you see the features you were hoping to? Did the GPS behave and did you identify any little wrinkles that you need to sort out before your next walk?

2 Take your GPS out onto the hill with a companion, and ask him to identify features on the ground you can navigate to. If he keeps the final destination a secret and you can correctly navigate to it by GPS you're doing well.

CHAPTER 5

Advanced Navigation with a GPS

Having looked at the basics it's time to move on to some more advanced techniques. We'll take a look at retracing your route (back-tracking) against setting a course that will take you straight back to your start point. We'll consider downloading routes and planning your own, and finally what to do when you take your GPS abroad.

Tracing your route

As discussed earlier, GPSs can not only tell you where you should be going, but also record where you have been. This could, of course, end up by being the same – but it doesn't have to be. You might have planned your route and entered the waypoints in advance. You then embark on the walk and at one particular point decide that you want to explore an interesting little valley you see off your route. You set off, have a look round and then decide to continue your route using the screen information on the GPS to get you back on route. At the completion of the walk, your planned route and the course you've walked will be different, as illustrated by Figure 5.1. The yellow band is the planned route, and the red line shows the actual route walked.

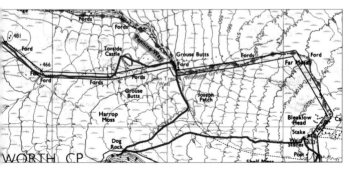

Figure 5.1 Screen grab of planned route and walked route

The ability of the GPS to record your walked route is an important one. Mountain rescue teams use GPSs to record where they've searched so they can check that no areas have been missed, and many people download their walked routes onto their digital mapping software (see Chapter 7) to store for future use.

One oft-cited use of a GPS for 'consumer' purposes is the ability, if things get tricky, to retrace your route back to the start – sometimes called backtracking. Different GPS units require different steps to enable this; check your user manual.

Once you've worked out how to do this you may discover you don't need to study the GPS too closely as you'll recognise the route you took. However, let's just consider how many times we've ever had to retrace our steps on a walk? I can only think of two occasions when I've gone back over a short section of a route when someone left something behind, but to retrace the entire route? Never.

What is more likely is that you reach a point on the walk where you feel it is unlikely that you will complete the planned route, and so you have to decide what to do next. The chances of you going back the way you've come, as already stated, are slim; adapting your current route to something more realistic is highly likely.

1   Study the map carefully and decide on a suitable route.
2   Identify a few key locations on this new route and enter their grid references into your GPS as new waypoints.
3a   Set up your new waypoints as a new route, activate it and then walk the route or
3b   Set your GPS to find the next waypoint, walk to it, then choose the next waypoint and so on until you reach your destination.

If your GPS is one that boasts OS mapping on screen, I would still advise you to study your route on a paper map first – even the largest screen doesn't have a big enough display to enable you to weigh up all the possible options. Of course you can zoom out to see a larger area of map, but this comes at the cost of display clarity, which you need in order to work out the best route. Use the map, and then transfer your route to your GPS.

Figures 5.2a–d It's possible to zoom in and out of your map on screen, but this results in either a loss of clarity or map area.

Figure 5.2a

Figure 5.2b

Figure 5.2c

Figure 5.2d

Downloading routes

There are many websites offering the opportunity to download routes onto your GPS. (A search on 'GPS routes download walking' on Google has just shown up 66,000, for example.) Some of these are paid-for services, others are currently free or have free samples available.

Finding a suitable route that fulfils all your needs is going to be a challenge; and once you've found one there's normally a slightly involved process to get it onto your GPS. This process isn't for the faint-hearted, but your ownership of a GPS assumes you are probably reasonably technical. You may also have to download additional software. The following are the steps required to get a route from the *Country Walking* route database onto your GPS. (At the time of writing you are restricted to GPSs which link to your computer with a serial cable – USB links are not supported.)

Figure 5.3
Screen grab from the Country Walking website

1 Log on to **www.countrywalkingroutes.co.uk** and click on the Routes menu.
2 Choose a suitable route (for this exercise choose a free route and one that shows the GPS icon).
3 You'll need to register (free) on the site to access the data.
4 Install the 'Save to GPS' software.
5 Attach your GPS to the serial port of your computer using the supplied cable, and set the GPS to receive data.
6 Click on the Start button and the route will be downloaded.

Other websites give you access to databases of waypoints, including mountain summits as well as downloadable routes. Again the steps to get them onto your GPS are many and varied. Some sites require extra software to convert the information into data your GPS can read; others only work on some makes of GPS. Some websites are listed in Appendix I, but keeping up-to-date in a printed book is impossible.

Let's pause again and reflect. If you've read my other two books on navigation you'll know my feelings on guidebooks and magazine routes. They are a great source of information written by people who know the area and so, as a starting point for your exploration, a good resource. However, sticking slavishly to guidebook routes always strikes me as a strange way of proceeding. I would always adapt the routes to suit my own needs of time and length and what I wanted to see. I transfer the route onto a map then work from there, adding or removing sections accordingly.

The same criticisms (and more) apply to those who download routes onto their GPSs and then follow them to the letter. Why greater criticism? There are two reasons. The first is that by putting the data straight onto your GPS you are not looking at the route on the map and so are unable to customise it. By all means run through the above exercise to see how it works, but don't get into the habit of doing it. My second criticism comes back to the old computer warning of GIGO – 'Garbage In, Garbage Out'. Books and magazine routes have been compiled by authors and publishers who have a vested interest in getting them as correct as humanly possible. Web-based routes do not necessarily get the same scrutiny. Although site owners want you to return, they may not be able to check everything that gets uploaded to their sites. Proceed with caution.

> *Practical exercise*
> Identify one of the many GPS-route websites. Download a route to your GPS and follow it. How was that? Was it as satisfying as planning the route yourself? Did you know where you were during the walk? Did you feel that the GPS was too much in charge of your destiny? What would have happened if the GPS had failed? Would you have been able to complete the route or get yourself off the hill?

Pre-planning

The general selling point on many of the route download sites is the amount of work you'll save by not having to enter the waypoints yourself. Once you've struggled your way through the steps required on some sites you may begin to question this!

Surely part of the fun of walking is in the planning of the route, the viewpoints, the refreshment stops? Figure 5.4 shows a route card template (downloadable from **www.navigationcourses.co.uk** and **www.cicerone.co.uk**). This format has worked very well for me over the years, and as well as containing much of the important information needed for a successful walk gets you thinking of a walk as a series of short sections or legs.

Taking each of the columns in turn, the From and To columns are just that. Identify the starting and finishing points of each of your legs, note the grid reference and a description or the name of the feature. The Magnetic Bearing column doesn't always need to be filled in, but until you get used to preparing route cards it's best to include it. Then we have the Height Climbed and Distance columns. The first involves counting the number of ascending contours you cross, and the second requires you to measure the horizontal distance

ROUTE CARD						Who is in the group?		Your contact details	
Date									
From (Grid Ref and Name)	To (Grid Ref and Name)	Magnetic Bearing	Height Climbed (m)	Distance (km)	Time Taken (mins)			Notes	
Alternative Route(s)				km	minutes	Where we are staying			
						Magnetic Variation for year _____ is _____ ° W or E			

Figure 5.4 Route card template

of the leg. The Time Taken column uses Naismith's formula (see Chapter 3) to calculate the time to walk the section.

> **Note** the reference to magnetic bearings; get into the habit of adding the magnetic variation (MV) to any compass bearing you take (see Chapter 3).

The final column is a useful reminder of why you made a particular decision when you planned the route. If you're leading a group, indicating planned breaks and loo stops can give your party the illusion that you've thought about their needs! The date, group members and contact details are useful reference, especially if you save the cards for future re-use. They are also vital safety features should your card be needed by a mountain rescue team. They'll know when you're walking the route, how many people to look for (and preferably their names) and have a way of contacting you.

The Alternative Route section bears a brief discussion as it is the section with which I have the most difficulty. Other authors have variously called this section Escape Routes, Emergency Routes or Bad Weather Routes, none of which I like. If you have good navigation skills bad weather shouldn't be an issue as you have the ability to navigate in any conditions; as for escape or emergency routes where do you plan these from? Does each leg require one, or do you plan an escape route from the most remote part of your walk? Whatever you plan, you can guarantee that any problems will occur anywhere other than at your escape point.

The only time I would use the alternative route section would be if I was planning a multi-day expedition where I might decide to walk a lower alternative route to get me out of the mountains in sustained bad weather.

Figure 5.5 shows a completed route card.

So what relevance does all this have to a GPS user? The simple answer is 'a great deal'. First and foremost it gets you thinking about the route with reference to the map. Even if your GPS has on-screen

ROUTE CARD Date	Edale to Snake Inn 2nd August 2007			Who is in the group? Pete, Dave, Paul and Annette		Your contact details 01298 111243
From (Grid Ref and Name)	To (Grid Ref and Name)	Magnetic Bearing	Height Climbed (m)	Distance (km)	Time Taken (mins)	Notes
Barber Booth - Tips Car Park 107 847	Upper Booth 103 853		30	1	18	Follow the road
Upper Booth 103 853	Top of Crowden Brook 094 873		410	2.25	75	Follow path by riverside
Top of Crowden Brook 094 873	Kinder Gates 088 887	335	40	2	34	Direct bearing or follow the rivers?
Kinder Gates 088 887	Kinder Downfall 083 889	302		0.6	9	Follow the river - lunchtime?
Kinder Downfall 083 889	Snake Path Junction 064 903	308 see notes	10	2.5	39	Follow edge path bearing 290 for 1 km then 317 for 1.5 km or direct bearing
Snake Path Junction 064 903	Snake Road Access Point 114 902			6	90	Follow stream side
Snake Road Access Point 114 902	Snake Inn 113 905		10	0.5	9	Finished! Time for a beer
Alternative Route(s)				14.85 kms kms	273 minutes minutes	Where we are staying Janet House B&B
						Magnetic Variation for 2007 is 3°W

© Pete Hawkins

Figure 5.5 Route card showing the proposed route and necessary information

OS maps you can't see enough of the landscape to plan a complete route adequately. Use the paper map to plan, and choose a walk that fits your criteria and requirements.

The planning process also enables you to iron out any problems in advance. The route may be too long or too short to suit your needs – if so, this is the opportunity to alter it before you load the information into the GPS.

So the route is now just right and it's time to enter the details into your GPS. The end points of each leg are the equivalent of GPS waypoints. The process of entering your route depends on the make of GPS, so check your instruction manual. Once finished and at the start of your route activate the route and you're away – a pre-planned route to follow on screen, with the route card and your map handy as back-up.

Practical exercise
Take a copy of the route card and plan a walk, then enter the details into your GPS. Walk the route, then compare the experience with the downloaded GPS route. I know which I prefer!

Using your GPS abroad

Taking your GPS abroad should be a straightforward process. Again you should always use it in conjunction with a map and the appropriate compass for where you are.

Silva compasses are balanced for three 'magnetic' zones – magnetic north, magnetic equator and magnetic south (Figure 5.6). If you use the wrong compass in a particular zone the needle won't swing freely and your bearings are likely to be inaccurate. The letters MN, ME or MS on the base of your compass housing denote the zone for which your compass is balanced.

Figure 5.6 Silva's three magnetic zones

The only adjustment you'll have to make is in resetting the grid system or map units the GPS uses. If you have set up your unit in England, Scotland or Wales correctly it should be set for OSGB or British Grid. You'll need to change this to match the grid system in use in the country you're in. You might see the correct system in your list on the GPS, or your local map may indicate which grid system it uses.

You're then free to use your GPS as you would in this country, but as you'll be using a non-British map you'll need to check it carefully for accuracy. Sadly few countries have maps as good as ours.

CHAPTER 6

Getting Out of Trouble

Throughout this book I have reminded you about the fallibility of your GPS. Batteries can fail, the unit can get damaged or wet, or can just freeze and refuse to work. If you've been relying on your GPS for your navigation you may suddenly find yourself in the middle of nowhere without a clue as to your location.

If you've followed my advice throughout earlier chapters you'll constantly refer to your map throughout the day, and so a failed GPS will only be a minor annoyance as you revert to your map (and compass) skills to continue the route. If you haven't been checking there are a number of techniques you could employ to get yourself out of trouble.

Checking your GPS

First check your GPS. If the batteries have run out you've no doubt got a spare set in your backpack. If the unit has frozen up try switching it off and on. If this fails try taking out the batteries, putting them back in and switching on again.

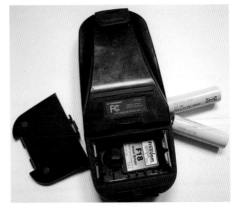

Figures 6.1a & b
Photo battery compartments. Note how both these GPSs take additional memory cards onto which your routes and waypoints are downloaded (Chapter 7)

Figure 6.1b

If your unit has become waterlogged, has stopped working or has just broken, you have fewer options. Keeping your GPS in a warm pocket with the batteries removed and the battery compartment cover left off may help it dry out, but it'll be a long process and it's probably not worth expecting it to work again that day.

Relocating yourself

So it's back to old-fashioned navigation. The first thing to do is to work out your position. Hopefully you have been alert to your general location throughout the walk and can identify a few landmarks. A couple of features will do at a push, three is ideal. Then follow these few steps:

1 Take out your compass and point the DOT arrow at your first feature.

2 Turn the compass housing round until the housing arrow and the north end of the needle coincide.

3 Read the bearing next to the DOT arrow and then subtract the magnetic variation (assuming magnetic north is west of grid north, as in the UK at the moment; where it's east of grid north – North America for example – add the MV on to your bearing.)

4 Take the map out, place the edge of the compass on the feature and rotate the compass around the feature until the housing arrow points north and the orienting lines are parallel to the vertical grid lines (Figure 6.2a).

5 Draw a thin pencil line along the edge of your compass.

6 Repeat this process for your other features. You should how have a single point on the map where all three lines cross, or (more likely) a small triangle, known as the Triangle of Error. You will be located somewhere inside the centre of the triangle (Figure 6.2b).

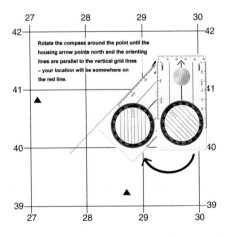

Figure 6.2a & b Using map and compass to relocate yourself

Figure 6.2b

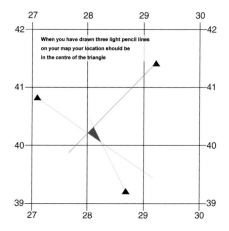

When you have drawn three light pencil lines on your map your location should be in the centre of the triangle

Practical exercise

Sit on top of a hill and identify three features around you. Run through the relocation exercise above to see if your current location is inside the triangle of error.

Aiming off

Once you have narrowed your location down to this small area you're probably OK to continue with your walk, or work out a route that will get you off the hill to safety. You may prefer to navigate to a known and identifiable point on the ground. You could, of course, aim directly for it, but as you don't know your exact location it is advisable to aim to miss the feature on purpose – a technique known as 'aiming off'. Look for a suitable feature, like a wall junction, and take a bearing to one side. Add on the magnetic variation and then follow the bearing until you reach the wall; turn and walk along the wall until you reach the junction. You are now at a known location and can continue your walk from there.

Figure 6.3
Aiming off:
aim to miss
deliberately!

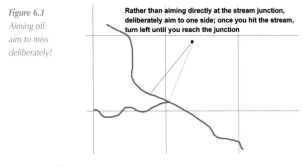

Rather than aiming directly at the stream junction, deliberately aim to one side; once you hit the stream, turn left until you reach the junction

Don't panic

The important thing is not to panic. Take time to reassess your situation and take rational decisions. It is very easy to think you know where you are, or make hasty or silly decisions which are only going to end you up in deeper holes. Many walkers desperately look for somewhere on the map where they may be and ignore any ground features which don't match, muttering 'Oh the map [or ground] must be wrong' to persuade themselves they're OK! Time spent getting it right now is only going to benefit you later on.

The main lesson learned from this chapter is continually to refer to your changing location on a paper map and not to rely on the GPS. Admittedly 99 percent of the time it'll work fine: but the 1 percent it fails will almost certainly be when conditions are poor and you're in a remote spot in failing light. Get it right from the outset and you'll avoid problems when you're tired and emotional.

> *Practical exercise*
> Plan a GPS walk and follow its instructions for a while. Then turn it off and try to work out where you are, and where you would go next. Could you navigate without your GPS? If the answer is 'No' your map and compass skills need more practice! If you decide to abandon the route where would you go?

CHAPTER 7

Computer Mapping Software

It's time to consider another aspect of the technological revolution that has hit the outdoor world recently: digital mapping. The Ordnance Survey's decision to license their mapping in digital form has been one of the most significant advances made by the organisation for years.

The maps come as part of software packages through which you can interact with the maps. There are four packages currently on the market – Tracklogs, Memory Map, Anquet and Fugawi – who all sell maps covering the whole of Great Britain at 1:50,000 and 1:25,000 scales. There are also other companies selling maps with limited coverage. These software packages, whilst all offering something slightly different, have one basic tenant: they enable you to access the digitised maps and to overlay your own information, such as waypoints and routes. These in turn can be linked to your GPS to upload routes you plan to walk or download routes you have walked and wish to review on-screen.

The software is currently only available to either PC users or Intel Mac users who can run Windows via Boot Camp or some other emulation programme. I have successfully run the software via Parallels emulation software on the Mac, although there are challenges getting routes up- and downloaded via Intel Macs. I have managed to get them to run on a PPC Mac via Guest PC but it goes very slowly – unless you have unlimited patience it really isn't worth trying!

Once your software of choice is up and running and you've loaded your map data you'll be presented with an on-screen map along with various other options. This book cannot teach you how to use your software – study the on-screen help and play around with it; the programmes aren't difficult to master. What we'll cover here is the way that digital maps can assist your on-hill navigation and pre-walk planning.

Instant exploration

One of the greatest joys of using digital mapping is its instant availability. Different programmes offer slightly different features, but by
entering a grid reference or place name you can instantly move to
that location on-screen (providing you have bought the map licence
to the area in question). Once you are centred on your desired location you can move the map around with the hand or movement
cursor to see the area to either side. You can zoom in (particularly
useful if you are trying to work out a tricky section of route) and out,
and even switch to aerial photographs if you have these loaded.

Assuming you have a reasonably up-to-date computer, moving about
the map should be fairly speedy. The on-screen clarity is superb (unless
you zoom too far in to the map and the image becomes pixelated).

Note Remember that as you zoom in you're not seeing any more
detail – all you're getting is a larger image size.

Practical exercise
Open up your software and play! The best way to familiarise yourself with the workings of any software is to spend time messing
around with it, working out what all the menus do, what the icons
are, etc. You can't break it (if it crashes, just relaunch and start again).

Getting in shape

One of the main advantages of digital mapping comes when you're
looking at the shape of the ground; contours are one of the most difficult aspects of map reading to come to terms with. If you're looking
at a map section with lots of features, the contours are invariably the
ones that disappear first; the pale brown lines will be obscured very
easily. Being able to look at the contours and understand the shape
of the ground is a difficult but incredibly useful skill to acquire.
Digital maps have made this much easier.

Practical exercise

Scroll the map to the area you want to examine. Take a close look at the contours and try to work out what landform you're looking at – a valley, a ridge, an escarpment (a hill with a steep slope on one side and a gentle one on the other)? Look for other clues on the map – streams or place names – in addition to the contours. Once you've decided what you're looking at click on the 3D button and the landscape will grow before your very eyes. (See the examples in Figure 7.1 – did you get it right?) Try it on a number of different landforms until you reach the point where you can look at a flat map and quickly pick up the shape of the land.

Figures 7.1 1a–4b Flat and 3D versions of various landforms
(3D images courtesy of Tracklogs Digital Mapping Software)

Figures 7.1 1a & b
The rounded valley of Bretton Brook with the sharp drop of Eyam Edge in the foreground

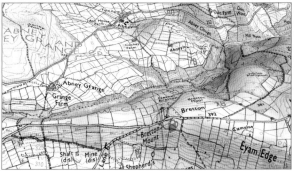

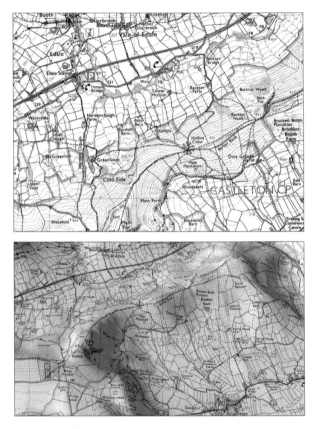

Figures 7.1 2a & b
The Mam Tor–Losehill ridge becomes much more obvious in 3D
Figures 7.1 3a & b *(Facing page) The eastern end of the Kinder Scout plateau: the many small stream valleys that eat away at the plateau edge stand out, but note that Kinder's famous small groughs don't show up; at less than 10m deep they're not visible with this map's contour interval*

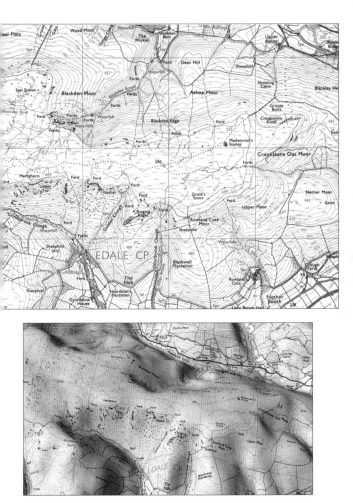

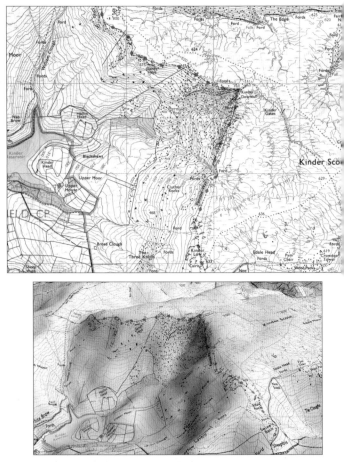

Figures 7.1 4a & b The Kinder downfall: flick your eyes between the two versions and the contour patterns of the flat plan become more obvious

Drawing routes

Once you have an idea of the shape of the ground it's time to start planning a few routes. Digital mapping, in theory, makes this a simple process. Activate the route-drawing option and then draw your intended route on screen. You'll notice that wherever you click your mouse you'll get a waypoint, and depending on the complexity of the route you may end up with dozens of them. If you were to print out the route as a route card you'd end up with an incomprehensible mass of figures.

It is possible to remove waypoints from your on-screen route, but before you do consider which points are needed and which aren't. Figure 7.2a is a map extract showing a manually planned route and Figure 7.2b its route card; the route has been kept short and simple, but the same principle applies for longer, more complex routes.

As you can see, it's a straightforward clockwise circuit of Stanton Moor. The route follows paths for most of the way except for one section where we need to follow a bearing from the path corner by the quarry to the Nine Ladies Stone circle. The starting point at Cork Stone isn't where the wording is but at the footpath junction by the disued New Park Quarry. The paths aren't straight, but neither are they complicated, so breaking the route down into the four legs illustrated in Figure 7.2b is a straightforward process.

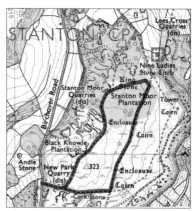

Figures 7.2a & b
Manual map extract and route card

ROUTE CARD	Stanton Moor					Your contact details	
Date	10th August 2007					01298 111243	
						Who is in the group? Pete, Annette, Steve and Clare	
From (Grid Ref and Name)	To (Grid Ref and Name)	Magnetic Bearing	Height Climbed (m)	Distance (km)	Time Taken (mins)		Notes
Cork Stone 243 627	Corner of Quarry 246 634		5	0.9	14		Follow path that leads north from Stone
Corner of Quarry 246 634	Nine Ladies Stone Circle 249 634	76		0.25	4		Take a bearing from quarry corner
Nine Ladies Stone Circle 249 634	Path junction 246 627		5	1	:6		Follow south-running path
Path junction 246 627	Roadside 242 628		10	0.5	9		Take path that runs west
Alternative Route(s)				2.65 kms kms	42 minutes minutes	Where we are staying Janet House B&B	
						Magnetic Variation for 2007 is 3°W	

© Pete Hawkins

Figure 7.2b Route card

Figure 7.3a is the same route drawn on screen, and Figure 7.3b its route card. In order to follow the paths on the ground it's been necessary to create a series of extra waypoints (the small blue dots in Figure 7.3a); the resultant route card (Figure 7.3b) now has nine legs (and 10 waypoints) and makes the whole process much more complicated than necessary.

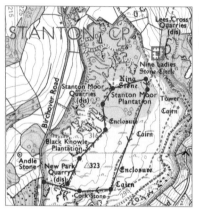

Figure 7.3a & b
On-screen planned route and route card

So how do you simplify the route for a GPS to follow? As we've discussed GPSs follow straight lines, and the leg from the start to the quarry corner doesn't follow a single straight line. You could get away with a straight line between waypoints 1 and 3, and points 3 and 5, but not between 1 and 5 (as on the manually planned route card) because you'll end up falling into two disused quarries.

The stretch from 5 to 6 is a straight line bearing whether manually planned or on-screen. The next section (from 6 to 7) on the ground is a short walk from the stone circle to the path. If you're trimming down waypoints a straight line from 6 to 8 is fine, and likewise from 8 to 10. The process of trimming this short route has reduced 10 legs to five, but it's still longer than the manually planned route.

Leg	Name / Position / Elevation	Bearing (given in degrees from True north)	Distance	Ascent	Time (mins)	Author Comments	Manual Waypoint number
	WP0301 SK 24345 62783 315 m					Starting point at Cork Stone	1
1	WP0302 SK 24430 62960 320 m	25	197m	6 m	6		
2	WP0303 SK 24630 63155 312 m	46	279m	0 m	3		
3	WP0304 SK 24600 63323 310 m	350	170m	0 m	1		
4	WP0305 SK 24678 63433 307 m	35	135m	0 m	1	Path bend by quarry	2
5	WP0306 SK 24905 63495 297 m	74	236m	0 m	2	Nine Ladies Stone Circle	3
6	WP0307 SK 24910 63420 299 m	176	75.2m	0 m			
7	WP0308 SK 24658 62758 304 m	201	709m	8 m	8	Path junctions	4
8	WP0309 SK 24443 62745 312 m	266	215m	8 m	3		
9	WP0310 SK 24193 62803 304 m	283	257m	2 m	2	Walk end by roadside	end
		Total	2.27km		26		

Figure 7.3b Route card

Figure 7.4

*Actual route recorded
by GPS*

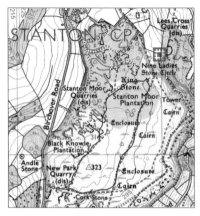

Figure 7.4 shows how a GPS recorded the route when it was actually walked (the track). The most interesting section is around the quarry to the left of the word 'Enclosure'. Despite following the path at this stage, the GPS recorded a suicidal trot into the quarries. The section across to the Nine Ladies followed a vague path on the ground so wasn't the straight line bearing that was planned. The track mostly followed our planned route for the rest of the walk, with only a few minor discrepancies.

Your mapping software can also do other things which you may find more or less useful, or just fun to play with. It is possible to fly through the landscape along your route using either your maps or the aerial photos as the backdrop – I'd classify this in the fun category. You can see the profile of the walk (Figure 7.5) and move your cursor along the route and see your location on the profile (or vice versa) – again more fun than telling you anything useful (though seeing all the ups and downs in advance may put you off doing the walk! (The profile in Figure 7.5 looks quite varied, but you're actually climbing no more than 10m in any one section.) Remember also that the vertical and horizontal scales will be set to fit the graph on-screen, so comparing the ups and downs of two routes may not be as straightforward as it might first appear. Looking at the route in 3D (Figure 7.6) helps to reinforce your understanding and appreciation of contours.

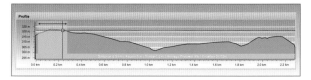

Figure 7.5 Profile of the Stanton Moor route

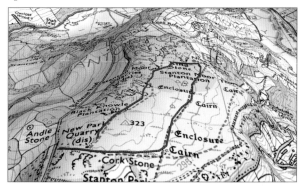

Figure 7.6 3D version of the Stanton Moor route (3D image courtesy of Tracklogs Digital Mapping Software)

Before we move on let's briefly consider why you would want to simplify your route. So long as your GPS has the capacity for lots of waypoints, then you can simply walk with the many-waypointed walk and your GPS will interpret the route for you. However, if you are following a complicated route then you'll be forever having to refer to your GPS and will be bombarded with arrival notifications as you reach your next waypoint. Spending a bit of time simplifying the route may make your walk more pleasurable.

A word of caution. Unless you are in access land as defined by the 2000 Countryside and Rights of Way Act (shown by a pale brown

shading and orange border on your OS 1:25000 map), or have the
permission of the landowner, you must stick to rights of way at all
times. In the Stanton Moor example – which is in access land – you
can walk in a straight line between points 1 and 3 and 3 and 5. If this
wasn't in access land you'd have to follow the path.

Practical exercise
Draw a route on-screen and see how easy you find the process –
it's all in the mouse control. If you make a mistake can you undo
it? Fancy extending the route? Can you work out how this is done?

Linking your GPS to your computer

As anyone who has suffered at the hands of emerging technologies
will testify, the rapid pace of change means we often buy a product
only to find that we can't use it as freely as we would like.
Traditionally the only way to link a GPS with a computer was via a
serial connector. More modern units have changed this to a USB
lead, and in some cases a removable disc to which routes and
waypoints are loaded via a card reader on your computer before

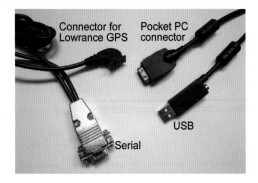

Figures 7.7
A variety
of GPS-to-
computer
connection
options

Connector for Lowrance GPS

Pocket PC connector

USB

Serial

transferring to the memory of your GPS (and vice versa). The loss of the serial connector has been spurred by the phasing out of these ports on modern computers, but not all mapping software can link to GPSs via USB and, as we have seen, neither can some route download sites.

If you already own a GPS and want to buy some digital mapping check your unit is compatible (and vice versa if you already own the software). Ask in shops, online help forums and technical support sections of the manufacturers' websites.

Once you have managed to connect your GPS to your computer and got the software to recognise it, it will (if it can pick up a signal) reveal your current location on screen. However as most of us use computers indoors this is a dubious advantage!

Linking the two together is genuinely useful for up- and downloading routes to and from your computer.

From computer to GPS and back again

Figure 7.8 Downloading screen

With your GPS and computer connected, it is now possible to download your planned route to your GPS, activate the route and set off on your planned walk using whatever technique you prefer to follow your route. Whilst on your walk, the GPS will record your actual route, as discussed previously. Once back home you can transfer your track (route that you walked) back onto the computer.

Transferring your route from GPS to computer

The process is pretty straightforward once you've managed to do it in reverse. The result is a coloured line on your on-screen map showing where you have walked (see Figure 7.5). As a way of archiving your route, and even making routes available to friends or Internet users via your website or the growing number of GPS route websites, this is a useful

Figure 7.9 Uploading screen

feature. It is also a good way of checking out where you went wrong if you strayed off course during the walk.

Note At the end of your walk switch off the route-recording function of your GPS. I always forget and so my trip home is recorded too, requiring extensive editing to remove the road element.

It is important to ensure that you do more than just upload your route. The waypoints will need labelling, as will the route to avoid confusing two routes in the future. There is also a growing trend to attach grid references to digital photos (Geotagging) and either append them to your existing mapping software or upload them to personal websites with links through to online mapping sites like Google maps. All achievable if you're prepared to spend time at your computer linking photos to your walked route.

Let's get back to downloading your route to your computer! I've read GPS articles that expound the virtues of downloading your route to check where you've been. That sounds pretty much like the occasional large party of ramblers I bump into in the Peak District, where the bunch towards the back are invariably nattering away without a clue where they are and what they've seen along the way! The 'see where you've been' facility suggests you've done the same and have walked blindly through the countryside oblivious to your route and surroundings. I hope not!

Digital maps are superb resources for walkers and give immense pleasure to mapophiles like me. Used with your GPS they add an extra dimension to walking and certainly make it easier to load routes into GPS units than the laborious manual method. If you're serious about wanting to use your GPS properly you're almost obliged to increase your set-up costs by adding some form of mapping software.

Open-source and non-Windows software

There are also many non-commercial software programmes available which have been written with GPSs in mind. A search on the Internet as I was writing this passage revealed millions of references, the most useful of which sent me to some fairly user-unfriendly websites designed and written by the technically minded for other technically minded folk. Most of it was way beyond me (and, I suspect, for the majority of outdoor devotees who use a GPS).

If you use a non-Windows computer you're going to be faced with a few challenges up- and downloading routes. I have managed to load a route I walked onto a Google map on my Apple Mac using a donation-ware programme called Trailrunner. It isn't an easy process, and planning a route in rural areas is far from straightforward on account of the programme's lack of decent maps. I have also come across an embryonic company called Routebuddy (**www.route-buddy.com**), which is hoping to add OS mapping capabilities to their existing software in the near future.

Until the established software companies start to adapt their programmes for non-Windows users you'll spend many a frustrating hour trying to find something that approximates to the current Windows-based programmes.

CHAPTER 8

Developing your GPS Skills

The growth in GPS ownership has seen the resurgence of a pastime that was for years restricted to Dartmoor. In pre-GPS years letterboxing was practised by a few hardy souls who would scour the moor looking for hidden boxes. Inside the box is a rubber stamp and a visitor's book. The finder, who has to solve a clue to find the box, stamps his book and leaves his own stamp in the visitor's book.

The sport started in 1854 when James Perrott of Chagford placed a glass jar in a small cairn at Cranmere Pool in the heart of the moor, in which visitors could leave their business cards. It took a while to catch on – the fifth box was only put out in 1962 – but the latter half of the last century saw a rapid growth in boxes and participants (see **www.dartmoorletterboxing.org**).

Figure 8.1 The official geocaching website

Figure 8.2a & b
A geocache location (a – above)
and cache (b – right)

The 21st-century version of letter-boxing is geocaching. The sport started with the switching off of 'selective availability' (see Chapter 1) – suddenly GPSs were more accurate, and after Internet forum discussions people started to hide objects and publicise their locations on the Internet. The rest, as they say, is history, and there are now Tupperware and similar boxes hidden all over the world just waiting for you to find them.

The idea is simple. Enter the location into your GPS and use it to locate the item. There are clues or hints to each location, and if you choose an area holding a number of caches you might be able to make a decent day's walk out of it. It could also be a great way to get children interested in walking. The geocaching website (**www.geocaching.com**) has links to caches around the world – be careful it doesn't turn into an obsession!

Practice makes perfect

Anyone who has played with a new piece of technology then put it away for a few weeks only to discover they've forgotten how to use it will understand the value of regular practice. Even with conventional map and compass work frequent practice is vital to ensure that when you need to use your skills you haven't forgotten them.

The GPS is no exception. Hopefully by now you have progressed beyond the 'switching on for a grid reference' level and are using your unit for something nearer to what the manufacturer intended. If you want your GPS to work for you in tricky conditions you must ensure your skills haven't become rusty, and practise them regularly via the exercises given in this book.

Don't lose sight of why you started walking in the first place: I'm sure it wasn't because of the existence of the GPS. Walking came first, and always should. Never lose an appreciation of where you are in the landscape, and never get so hooked on your GPS that you don't look around and use common sense in navigation. Your GPS may be taking you in a straight line from A to B, but if you can see on the ground that the path isn't straight, follow the path. Your GPS will 'bring' you back to your destination anyway, so there's no chance of getting lost.

Your GPS is a great tool to help you get the most out of your walking. Like a map and compass it can be invaluable, but never let it obscure the reason you're out there in the first place. Read the ground as much as your GPS and you will continue to get the same amount of pleasure as when you started walking – only now you should know where you are most of the time, and not spend valuable walking time scratching your head and wondering! Enjoy your GPS – but enjoy your walking more.

Notes on using the free GPS navigation aid

There are various elements to the GPS navigation aid, and the following information should help you use it to the full:

- The compass rose can be used to check quickly a bearing from your current location to the next. Place the central cross on your location and read off your grid bearing against the edge of the rose. (The subdivisions are marked every 2°.)

- Use the Romers (1:25,000 and 1:50,000 scales) to provide an accurate grid reference before entering the data into your GPS for your next waypoint. Remember which way round grid references are read (Chapter 3), and that a six- or (at a push) eight-figure reference is adequate, despite the GPS's ability to give a 10-figure reference.

- Use the two scales to measure distances on your map.

- Note the reminder of what to do should your GPS fail. Above all don't panic.

APPENDIX I
Further Information

Training Courses
Map and compass courses run by the author:
Silva Map and Compass Courses
Jaret House B&B
Queen Street
Tideswell
Derbyshire SK17 8JZ
01298 872801
Email: info@navigationcourses.co.uk
www.navigationcourses.co.uk

Other map and compass courses:
www.nnas.org.uk National Navigation Award Scheme
www.silva.ltd.uk Silva UK

Useful Websites
http://www.geomag.bgs.ac.uk/navigation.html British Geological
Survey Magnetic Variation Calculator
www.nearby.org.uk Translates virtually any locational reference
(latitude and longitude, grid references, post codes and so on) into
others

Digital Mapping Companies
Tracklogs www.tracklogs.co.uk
Memory Map www.memory-map.co.uk
Fugawi www.fugawi.com
Anquet www.anquet.co.uk
Routebuddy www.routebuddy.com

GPS Manufacturers
Lowrance www.lowrance.com UK importers www.silva.ltd.uk
Magellan www.magellangps.com
Garmin www.garmin.com
Road Angel Navigator 7000 (with Memory Map mapping)
www.memory-map.co.uk
Mitac www.mio-tech.be Makers of the now obsolete Mitac Mio 168
Pocket PC PDA with inbuilt GPS
SatMap www.satmap.com

GPS Route Websites
Phil's GPS Mountain Resources www.haroldstreet.org.uk
Go4awalk www.go4awalk.com
UK Walking webring b.webring.com/hub?ring=walkingbritainne
Walking World www.walkingworld.com
Share My Routes www.sharemyroutes.com
Country Walking www.countrywalkingroutes.co.uk
Walk with GPS www.walk-with-gps.co.uk
Grab your Boots www.grabyourboots.com

APPENDIX II
Further Reading

Map and Compass: The art of navigation Pete Hawkins (Cicerone, 2003)

Navigation: Techniques and skills for walkers Pete Hawkins (Cicerone, 2007)

Hillwalking Steve Long (Mountain Leader Training, 2004)

Mountain Weather: A practical guide for hillwalkers and climbers in the British Isles David Pedgley (Cicerone, 2006)

The Hillwalker's Manual Bill Birkett (Cicerone, 2002)

INDEX

NOTES

Get ready for take off

Adventure Travel helps you to go outdoors over there

More ideas, information, advice and entertaining features on overseas trekking, walking and backpacking than any other magazine - guaranteed.

Available from good newsagents or by subscription - 6 issues £15

Adventure Travel Magazine T:01789-488166

SAVE £££'s with

THE GREAT OUTDOORS

Britain's leading monthly magazine for the dedicated walker. To find out how much you can save by subscribing call

0141 302 7744

HILLWALKING • BACKPACKING • TREKKING • SCRAMBLING

LISTING OF CICERONE GUIDES

AFRICA

Climbing in the Moroccan Anti-Atlas
Kilimanjaro
Trekking in the Atlas Mountains

THE ALPS (WALKING AND TREKKING)

100 Hut Walks in the Alps
Across the Eastern Alps: E5
Alpine Points of View
Alpine Ski Mountaineering
   Vol 1 Western Alps
Alpine Ski Mountaineering
   Vol 2 Eastern Alps
Chamonix to Zermatt
Snowshoeing: Techniques and Routes
   in the Western Alps
Tour of the Matterhorn
Tour of Mont Blanc
Tour of Monte Rosa
Walking in the Alps (all Alpine areas)

CROATIA AND SLOVENIA

Julian Alps of Slovenia
Walking in Croatia

EASTERN EUROPE

High Tatras
Mountains of Montenegro
Mountains of Romania
Walking in Hungary

FRANCE, BELGIUM AND LUXEMBOURG

Cathar Way
Ecrins National Park
GR5 Trail
GR20 Corsica – The High Level
   Route
Mont Blanc Walks
RLS (Robert Louis Stevenson) Trail
Rock Climbs Belgium and
   Luxembourg
Tour of the Oisans: GR54
Tour of the Vanoise
Trekking in the Vosges and Jura
Vanoise Ski Touring
Walking in the Cathar region
   of south west France
Walking in the Cevennes
Walking in the Dordogne
Walking in the Haute Savoie, Vol 1
Walking in the Haute Savoie, Vol 2
Walking in the Languedoc
Walking in Provence
Walking in the Tarentaise and
   Beaufortain Alps
Walking on Corsica
Walking the French Gorges
Walks in Volcano Country

GERMANY AND AUSTRIA

Germany's Romantic Road
King Ludwig Way
Klettersteig Scrambles in
   Northern Limestone Alps
Mountain Walking in Austria
Trekking in the Stubai Alps
Trekking in the Zillertal Alps
Walking in the Bavarian Alps
Walking in the Harz Mountains
Walking in the Salzkammergut
Walking the River Rhine Trail

HIMALAYAS – NEPAL, INDIA, TIBET

Annapurna – A Trekker's Guide
Bhutan – A Trekker's Guide
Everest – A Trekkers' Guide
Garhwal & Kumaon –
   A Trekkers' Guide
Kangchenjunga – A Trekkers' Guide
Langtang, Gosainkund and
   Helambu: A Trekkers' Guide
Manaslu – A Trekkers' Guide
Mount Kailash Trek

ITALY

Central Apennines of Italy
Gran Paradiso
Italian Rock
Shorter Walks in the Dolomites
Through the Italian Alps: the GTA
Trekking in the Apennines
Treks in the Dolomites
Via Ferratas of the Italian
   Dolomites Vol 1
Via Ferratas of the Italian
   Dolomites Vol 2
Walking in the Central Italian Alps
Walking in the Dolomites
Walking in Sicily
Walking in Tuscany

NORTH AMERICA

Grand Canyon and American South
   West
John Muir Trail
Walking in British Columbia

OTHER MEDITERRANEAN COUNTRIES

Climbs and Treks in the Ala Dag
   (Turkey)
High Mountains of Crete
Jordan – Walks, Treks, Caves etc.
Mountains of Greece
Treks and Climbs Wadi Rum, Jordan
Walking in Malta
Walking in Western Crete

PYRENEES AND FRANCE / SPAIN

Canyoning in Southern Europe
GR10 Trail: Through the
   French Pyrenees
Mountains of Andorra
Rock Climbs in the Pyrenees
Pyrenean Haute Route
Pyrenees – World's Mountain Range
   Guide
Through the Spanish Pyrenees GR11
Walks and Climbs in the Pyrenees

Way of St James – Le Puy to
   the Pyrenees
Way of St James – Pyrenees-Santiago-
   Finisterre

SCANDINAVIA

Pilgrim Road to Nidaros
   (St Olav's Way)
Walking in Norway

SOUTH AMERICA

Aconcagua

SPAIN AND PORTUGAL

Costa Blanca Walks Vol 1
Costa Blanca Walks Vol 2
Mountains of Central Spain
Picos de Europa – Walks and Climbs
Via de la Plata (Seville To Santiago)
Walking in the Algarve
Walking in the Canary Islands 1 West
Walking in the Canary Islands 2 East
Walking in the Cordillera Cantabrica
Walking the GR7 in Andalucia
Walking in Madeira
Walking in Mallorca
Walking in the Sierra Nevada

SWITZERLAND

Alpine Pass Route
Bernese Alps
Central Switzerland –
   A Walker's Guide
Tour of the Jungfrau Region
Walking in Ticino, Switzerland
Walking in the Valais
Walks in the Engadine, Switzerland

INTERNATIONAL CYCLE GUIDES

Cycle Touring in France
Cycle Touring in Spain
Cycle Touring in Switzerland
Cycling in the French Alps
Cycling the River Loire – The Way
   of St Martin
Danube Cycle Way
Way of St James – Le Puy to Santiago
   cyclist's guide

MINI GUIDES

Avalanche!
GPS
Navigation
Pocket First Aid and Wilderness
   Medicine
Snow

TECHNIQUES AND EDUCATION

Adventure Alternative
Beyond Adventure
Hillwalker's Guide to Mountaineering
Hillwalker's Manual
Map and Compass
Mountain Weather
Outdoor Photography
Rock Climbing
Snow and Ice Techniques
Sport Climbing

Cicerone's mission is to inform and inspire by providing the best guides to exploring the world

Since its foundation over 30 years ago, Cicerone has specialised in publishing guidebooks and has built a reputation for quality and reliability. It now publishes nearly 300 guides to the major destinations for outdoor enthusiasts, including Europe, UK and the rest of the world.

Written by leading and committed specialists, Cicerone guides are recognised as the most authoritative. They are full of information, maps and illustrations so that the user can plan and complete a successful and safe trip or expedition – be it a long face climb, a walk over Lakeland fells, an alpine traverse, a Himalayan trek or a ramble in the countryside.

With a thorough introduction to assist planning, clear diagrams, maps and colour photographs to illustrate the terrain and route, and accurate and detailed text, Cicerone guides are designed for ease of use and access to the information.

If the facts on the ground change, or there is any aspect of a guide that you think we can improve, we are always delighted to hear from you.

Cicerone Press
2 Police Square Milnthorpe Cumbria LA7 7PY
Tel:01539 562 069   Fax:01539 563 417
e-mail:info@cicerone.co.uk   web:www.cicerone.co.uk

CICERONE